3-step
EXPRESS
meals

3-step

EXPRESS

meals

**easy
weeknight
recipes for
today's home
cook**

table of contents

WELCOME!

With hectic schedules and never-ending to-do lists, getting a healthy, home-cooked meal on the table every evening can be a challenge. We're all looking for shortcuts and simple solutions that fit into our fast-paced schedules but don't want to rely on takeout.

At *Cooking Light,* we've found you can get a meal on the table in just three easy steps. The keys to this fast meal prep are utilizing healthy convenience products that save time without sacrificing flavor or your health, relying on streamlined techniques and kitchen tools that allow you to multitask in the kitchen, and using fresh ingredients that make each dish sing. The built-in game plans within each recipe also help ensure you get the full meal on the table at once.

We'll show you how to stock your pantry with time-saving products—sauces for simmering, spices to add flavor to sautés, and meats that cook in minutes—and teach you the techniques we use to get healthy meals, sides included, on the table in three steps. You'll find recipe-specific Prep Tips to help you along the way and Simple Swap suggestions for tailoring the meals to suit your family's tastes or to use the ingredients you may have on hand. From mouthwatering main dishes to light and refreshing salads and sides, getting meals on the table is really as simple as 1-2-3.

—the editors of *Cooking Light*

1

EXPRESS

grocery store guide »

Learn how to stock your kitchen and streamline meal preparation to get healthy dinners on the table fast.

easy 3-step *EXPRESS* meals

Quick cooking isn't about sacrificing flavor, texture, and nutrition to a time-crunched schedule. The secret to mastering 3-step express meals is to stock your kitchen with the right ingredients on three fronts—the refrigerator, the freezer, and the pantry.

- - - - - - - - - -

The grocery store is filled with lots of ingredients and products that are designed to help you save time in the kitchen—the key is finding the ones that keep your healthy-eating goals intact without sacrificing flavor. Streamlined techniques and the built-in game plans in each recipe help ensure that you get a delicious meal on the table in three easy steps using healthy store-bought products and fresh ingredients that take minimal time to prepare. Here, you'll find smart buying, cooking, and preparation tips and our list of essentials for a well-stocked kitchen.

TEN TIPS

for preparing 3-step express meals

1 Buy fresh produce in season. Always start with fresh, peak-season ingredients, which often need the least help and fuss in the kitchen. Fresh peaches and summer berries are bursting with juice and sweetness, while fall apples are refreshingly crisp and full of flavor. When winter comes, commit to root vegetables and Brussels sprouts, and explore easy, flavor-enhancing techniques, such as roasting and broiling.

2 Keep things simple. Have the confidence to season simply. Fresh chicken will be delicious with just salt, freshly ground black pepper, and lemon rind. Summer tomatoes sparkle with a bit of oil, black pepper, and fresh herbs. Play with the idea of simplicity and restraint. Let the ingredients sing.

3 Let others do the work. Too few cooks take advantage of help at the store. Have the butcher cut, bone, or skin meat, and ask the fishmonger to skin or fillet the fish. Buy precut fruits and vegetables, too, if you need to save more time.

4 Utilize no-cook products. Explore the store for high-quality, no-cook proteins for pasta tosses, salads, pizzas, or sandwiches. Jarred sustainable tuna, rotisserie chicken, smoked pork, or smoked salmon or trout are just a few options that can help give you a jumpstart on dinner.

5 Use your freezer wisely. You can stock up on healthy freezer options (see page 13), but you can also label and store extra portions of sauces, sides, and entrées. That extra cup of pasta sauce will come in handy for pizza, meatball hoagies, or even soup on a particularly busy night.

6 Make sure your pan is hot. Quick cooking often involves searing fish, meat, or poultry and sautéing or stir-frying vegetables on the stovetop. A good pan, preheated until really hot, delivers the intense flavors and beautiful browned crusts you want.

7 Use your microwave. Utilizing the microwave helps you streamline prep and cut down on the pots and pans you have to clean later. You can quickly zap parchment-wrapped beets for a side, soften bell peppers to stuff, or bring stock to a boil for soup.

8 Do a bit of work on the weekends. On a lazy Sunday, make versatile, high-flavor components, such as roasted tomatoes, toasted breadcrumbs, and roasted garlic, to simplify cooking later in the week. You can also blanch vegetables. Here's how: Trim and boil green beans, cauliflower, butternut squash, or broccoli for a few minutes just to get them softened. Drain and shock in ice water, and then drain and store for the week. Or chop ahead. In a few minutes of downtime, you can get those onions, carrots, cauliflower, or broccoli prepped and ready to go. Store in airtight containers in the fridge.

9 Cook once, eat twice. If you're planning to grill four chicken breasts, grill eight to have four on hand. When roasting vegetables, do a giant batch—it adds little time on the front end. Use extras for salads, pizzas, tacos, and pastas.

10 Invest in good knives. You simplify prep greatly when you have sharp, precise knives and hone your knife skills. Simple, quick food, often sautéed or stir-fried, needs to be cut into the same size pieces; they're prettier, too. It's often much quicker and less messy to hand-cut than to yank out (and clean) the food processor.

STAPLES
of the 3-step express kitchen »

Pantry

○ **CANNED BEANS:** These are a true time-saver in the kitchen. Use organic or no-salt-added beans to help keep sodium levels in check, and rinse them after draining to reduce the sodium even more—by 40 percent. Toss them into salads, soups, and stews.

○ **CANNED BROTH:** Making homemade stock is a time-consuming process. Opt for fat-free, lower-sodium or lower-sodium organic varieties of beef, chicken, and vegetable broth. It's an easy switch from regular, and it's sure to reduce sodium.

○ **CANNED TOMATOES:** Crushed, diced, stewed, and whole tomatoes are helpful ingredients for the quick cook. You can also take advantage of various flavorings: fire-roasted tomatoes, tomatoes with basil, tomatoes and chiles. Opt for no-salt-added or organic varieties, if possible, for sodium savings.

○ **LOWER-SODIUM MARINARA SAUCE:** Use the rich, slow-simmered, herby flavor of marinara sauce as a starting point for an assortment of meals, from chili to baked pasta.

○ **CANNED OR JARRED FISH:** Shelf-stable seafood is an easy, often inexpensive time-saving option. With a few cans of water-packed sustainable tuna or salmon in your pantry, you have the makings of a tasty pasta or main-course salad. It often comes packed with added salt (200mg to 300mg sodium in 2 ounces), so choose the lower-sodium or unsalted variety, if available.

○ **PRECOOKED BROWN RICE:** We all need to eat more whole grains, but they're not exactly an easy choice for the fast cook—brown rice can take an hour to cook. Until now: Say "Hello" to precooked brown rice, which is cooked, and then put into a shelf-stable pouch with little added salt (i.e., it's not a sodium bomb) and takes 90 seconds or less to heat in the microwave. Instant and boil-in-a-bag rice are also good options; they're ready in 10 to 12 minutes on the stovetop.

○ **DRIED PASTAS:** Dried pastas are certainly convenient—they're ready in about 15 minutes—and have a satisfying chew when cooked al dente. Have a selection of your favorite shapes in the pantry—the smaller, thinner varieties cook more quickly. But when every minute counts, look for refrigerated fresh pasta (see page 13).

NUTS: Keep one or a few of your favorites—almonds, walnuts, pecans, pine nuts, pistachios, cashews—on hand to add to salads or sides, mix into quick breads, or toss on noodle dishes.

SAUCES: Reach for convenient, high-flavor ingredients, such as lower-sodium soy sauce, hoisin, Sriracha, and Worcestershire sauce to jazz up quick entrées.

OILS: You'll want to have canola oil and olive oil on hand for sautéing, stir-frying, and using in vinaigrettes and marinades. If you make Asian-inspired dishes with any frequency, you should purchase a small bottle of dark sesame oil.

VINEGARS: Have a couple types of vinegar on hand for seasoning and to use as a base for salad dressing—balsamic vinegar, red wine vinegar, white vinegar, and cider vinegar are flavorful options.

Refrigerator

PIZZA DOUGH: In the roster of shortcut ingredients, fresh pizza dough is an all-star. In as little as 30 minutes, you can make a fantastic pie with a crispy-chewy, deliciously browned crust, hot from the oven. And when you load it with fresh vegetables: Voilà, a wonderfully healthy veggie pizza. Fresh dough, from the supermarket bakery section or a local pizzeria, is our favorite to work with, though canned dough and prebaked crusts work fine in a pinch.

FRESH PASTAS: For those nights when you don't have the 15 minutes to cook dried fettuccine, reach for refrigerated fresh pasta: It's done in about a minute or two. The texture is deliciously different—more delicate, with a slightly springy bounce that can hold its own with rich sauces and bold ingredients.

REFRIGERATED POTATOES: Available in all forms—mashed, hashed, wedges—they simply need a quick warm-up in the microwave or oven. Look for brands that don't have added seasonings and salt—some can be full of saturated fat and sodium. Add your own seasonings like fresh herbs, garlic, horseradish, or freshly grated Parmesan.

PRECUT PRODUCE: You can't beat the convenience factor—some are even designed to microwave-steam in a bag. You can also spread veggies on a baking sheet to roast.

BAGGED LETTUCES: Rinsing, drying, stemming, and chopping supermarket spinach is a messy time-eater. Ready-to-use bags of greens cut out that whole process and come in a wide assortment—spinach, mixed baby greens, romaine, kale. Inspect the lettuce in the store to make sure it's in prime condition: no black spots, no wilting.

HUMMUS: This dip is the ringer in our shortcut lineup; it's far more versatile than you might think. It can be a tasty base for a wide range of easy, vegetable-packed sandwiches made special with the robust flavor of garlic and nutty tahini. And hummus is loaded with protein and fiber. There are lots of flavored varieties available, but you can also stir in your own flourishes, like lemon rind, hot sauce, crushed red pepper, chopped fresh herbs, or more fresh minced garlic.

PESTO: The garlicky, herb-kissed flavor of pesto is like nothing else. Refrigerated pesto (usually stocked near the fresh pasta in most grocery stores) is an easy way to add a punch of flavor to pastas, salads, sandwiches, pizzas, fish, and more.

ROTISSERIE CHICKEN: Supermarket rotisserie chicken—a moist, plump, savory bird just waiting for you to pick up and carry home—is a help to put in soups, stews, tacos, and casseroles. But it's equally handy kept in the fridge for tomorrow's quick salad meals. Stick with the original, unflavored version, as it's the most versatile.

LARGE EGGS: There's simply no protein that can be prepared as quickly as eggs, and in so many ways. Use them as a binder in patties and meatballs or to bulk up fried rice or hard boil them for use in salads.

Freezer

FROZEN VEGETABLES: Frozen veggies are ideal for getting dinner on the table in minutes. They retain not only their nutrients but also much of their sweet flavor. You can steam them in the microwave for a quick-cooking side or sauté with fresh herbs for an easy stovetop option.

FROZEN POTATOES: Unseasoned frozen potato wedges are another convenient option. You can add your own seasonings and garnishes. Or leave them plain and serve with mayonnaise with roasted garlic, pesto, or hot sauce stirred in for dipping.

PEELED AND DEVEINED SHRIMP: Frozen shrimp that have already been peeled and deveined are available in one-pound bags, saving you at least 10 minutes of prep. But this convenience can come at a nutritional cost. Peeled and "easy-peel" shrimp are usually soaked in a sodium solution. Check the label. You may need to adjust how you season the shrimp.

FROZEN FISH: Grocery stores often sell large packages of individually wrapped, frozen fish fillets, usually at a cost dramatically discounted from fresh varieties. You can also purchase in-season fresh fish, and freeze it for later.

2

poultry
& meat »

The healthy quick cook relies on the right lean cuts and proper technique to yield tender, succulent entrées.

SIMPLE SWAP *Make with turkey cutlets instead of chicken. Swap out fresh broccoli for broccoli rabe.*

Rosemary-Fig Chicken *and* Spicy Garlic Broccoli Rabe

HANDS-ON TIME: 26 min. **TOTAL TIME:** 30 min.

PREP TIP *This gorgeous dish is quick, easy, and unbeatable in terms of taste. Use garlic powder instead of fresh garlic; it won't burn when you sear the chicken.*

- 4 quarts water
- 1½ pounds broccoli rabe, trimmed
- 1 teaspoon garlic powder, divided
- ¾ teaspoon salt, divided
- ½ teaspoon freshly ground black pepper
- 4 (6-ounce) skinless, boneless chicken breast halves

- Cooking spray
- ⅔ cup fig preserves
- 1 tablespoon minced fresh rosemary
- 6 tablespoons port or other sweet red wine
- 1 tablespoon olive oil
- ¼ teaspoon crushed red pepper
- 2 teaspoons grated lemon rind

1 **Bring 4 quarts water to a boil** in a large Dutch oven. Add broccoli rabe to pan, and cook, uncovered, 5 to 6 minutes or until crisp-tender. Drain and plunge broccoli rabe into ice water; drain.

2 **While broccoli rabe cooks, heat a skillet** over medium-high heat. Sprinkle ½ teaspoon garlic powder, ½ teaspoon salt, and black pepper over chicken; coat with cooking spray. Add chicken to pan; cook 3 minutes on each side or until browned. Combine fig preserves, rosemary, and wine; add to chicken. Cover, reduce heat to medium, and cook 6 minutes or until done. Uncover and cook 1 minute or until sauce is slightly thick.

3 **While chicken cooks, heat a non-stick skillet** over medium heat. Add oil; swirl to coat. Combine ½ teaspoon garlic powder, ¼ teaspoon salt, and red pepper; add to pan. Add broccoli rabe; cook until heated. Sprinkle with rind; toss. Serves 4 (serving size: 1 chicken breast half, about 3 tablespoons sauce, and 1 cup broccoli rabe)

Calories 398; Fat 6g (sat 1.1g, mono 3g, poly 1g); Protein 44g; Carb 37.9g; Fiber 0.4g; Chol 99mg; Iron 2.4mg; Sodium 586mg; Calc 85mg

SIMPLE SWAP

This sauce will work equally well with chicken thighs or pork.

Maple-Mustard Glazed Chicken *with* Rice

HANDS-ON TIME: 15 min. **TOTAL TIME:** 30 min.

PREP TIP *Serve this tangy-sweet chicken with rice to soak up every last bit of the flavorful sauce. Pair it with a simple green salad or steam-in-bag green beans that can cook in the microwave while you prep the chicken.*

- 1 cup uncooked brown rice
- 2 teaspoons olive oil
- 4 (6-ounce) skinless, boneless chicken breast halves
- ½ teaspoon freshly ground black pepper
- ¼ teaspoon salt
- ¼ cup fat-free, lower-sodium chicken broth
- ¼ cup maple syrup
- 2 teaspoons chopped fresh thyme
- 2 medium garlic cloves, thinly sliced
- 1 tablespoon cider vinegar
- 1 tablespoon stone-ground mustard

1 **Preheat oven to 400°.** Cook rice according to package directions, omitting salt and fat.

2 **Heat a large ovenproof skillet** over medium-high heat. Add oil to pan; swirl to coat. Sprinkle chicken with pepper and salt. Add chicken to pan; sauté 2 minutes on each side or until browned. Remove chicken from pan. Add broth, syrup, thyme, and garlic to pan; bring to a boil, scraping pan to loosen browned bits. Cook 2 minutes, stirring frequently. Add vinegar and mustard; cook 1 minute, stirring constantly.

3 **Return chicken to pan;** spoon mustard mixture over chicken. Bake at 400° for 10 minutes or until chicken is done. Remove chicken from pan; let stand 5 minutes. Place pan over medium heat; cook mustard mixture 2 minutes or until liquid is syrupy. Serve with chicken. Serves 4 (serving size: 1 breast half, about 1 tablespoon sauce, and ½ cup rice)

Calories 373; Fat 5.2g (sat 1.1g, mono 2.5g, poly 1g); Protein 41.8g; Carb 37.1g; Fiber 2g; Chol 99mg; Iron 2.1mg; Sodium 338mg; Calc 48mg

Italian-Seasoned Roast Chicken Breasts

HANDS-ON TIME: 15 min. **TOTAL TIME:** 60 min.

PREP TIP *Lean breast meat needs to be shielded as it cooks, so leave the skin on. And, since chicken breast meat is low in calories and saturated fat, you can eat the skin and still keep saturated fat within allowable limits. Serve with sautéed spinach and mashed potatoes for a hearty meal. Prepare them while the chicken bakes.*

- 1 tablespoon chopped fresh rosemary
- 1 teaspoon grated lemon rind
- 2 tablespoons fresh lemon juice
- 4 teaspoons extra-virgin olive oil
- ½ teaspoon fennel seeds, crushed
- ½ teaspoon salt
- ¼ teaspoon freshly ground black pepper
- 3 garlic cloves, minced
- 4 bone-in chicken breast halves (about 3 pounds)
- Cooking spray

1 **Preheat oven to 425°.** Combine first 8 ingredients in a bowl, stirring well.

2 **Loosen skin from chicken** by inserting fingers, gently pushing between skin and meat. Rub rosemary mixture under loosened skin over flesh; rub over top of skin.

3 **Place chicken,** bone side down, on a broiler pan coated with cooking spray. Coat skin lightly with cooking spray. Bake at 425° for 35 minutes or until a thermometer inserted into the thickest portion of the breast registers 155°. Remove chicken from pan; let stand 10 minutes. Serves 4 (serving size: 1 chicken breast half)

Calories 240; Fat 12.2g (sat 2.8g, mono 6.3g, poly 2.1g); Protein 29.5g; Carb 1.8g; Fiber 0.3g; Chol 82mg; Iron 1.2mg; Sodium 366mg; Calc 24mg

SIMPLE SWAP

This blend of seasoning is delicious, but you can use any mix of fresh herbs or fresh lime in place of lemon.

Chicken-Butternut Tagine *and* Whole-Wheat Couscous

HANDS-ON TIME: 25 min. **TOTAL TIME:** 35 min.

PREP TIP *Serve this quick adaptation of the classic Moroccan dish over whole-wheat couscous to soak up some of the rich flavors. The couscous takes just five minutes to cook.*

1¼ cups water
¼ teaspoon salt
1 cup uncooked whole-wheat couscous
1 tablespoon olive oil
2 cups chopped onion
2 teaspoons ground cumin
1 teaspoon paprika
1 teaspoon ground turmeric
¼ teaspoon ground cinnamon
¼ teaspoon ground ginger

2 garlic cloves, minced
1 pound skinless, boneless chicken breast, cut into bite-sized pieces
2 cups fat-free, lower-sodium chicken broth
8 ounces cubed peeled butternut squash
⅓ cup halved pitted picholine olives (about 3 ounces)
8 pitted dried plums, chopped
Flat-leaf parsley leaves (optional)

1 **Bring 1¼ cups water** and ¼ teaspoon salt to a boil in a medium saucepan. Stir in couscous; cover. Remove pan from heat.

2 **While couscous stands, heat a Dutch oven** over medium heat. Add oil to pan; swirl to coat. Add onion; cook 8 minutes or until golden, stirring occasionally. Stir in cumin and next 6 ingredients (through chicken); cook 1 minute, stirring constantly.

3 **Stir in broth,** squash, olives, and dried plums; bring to a boil. Cover, reduce heat to medium-low; simmer 10 minutes or until squash is tender. Fluff couscous; serve with tagine. Garnish with parsley, if desired. Serves 4 (serving size: 1¼ cups tagine and ⅔ cup couscous)

Calories 479; Fat 9.3g (sat 0.9g, mono 5.3g, poly 1.6g); Protein 36.8g; Carb 66.7g; Fiber 11.2g; Chol 66mg; Iron 4.3mg; Sodium 710mg; Calc 110mg

Herbed Arugula-Tomato Salad *with* Chicken

HANDS-ON TIME: 35 min. **TOTAL TIME:** 35 min.

PREP TIP *Pair this Mediterranean-inspired salad with an easy side like garlic bread. You can place the bread under the broiler while you assemble the salads. It will take just a minute or two to toast.*

- 3 tablespoons extra-virgin olive oil, divided
- 1 teaspoon grated lemon rind
- 1 tablespoon fresh lemon juice
- 4 (4-ounce) chicken breast cutlets
- 2 cups halved cherry tomatoes
- 1 (5-ounce) package fresh baby arugula
- 1½ tablespoons white wine vinegar
- 1 teaspoon dried herbes de Provence
- ½ teaspoon Dijon mustard
- 1 garlic clove, minced
- ½ teaspoon salt, divided
- ½ teaspoon freshly ground black pepper, divided
- Cooking spray
- 3 tablespoons halved pitted kalamata olives

1 **Combine 1 tablespoon oil,** rind, juice, and chicken cutlets; let stand 5 minutes.

2 **While chicken stands, combine tomatoes** and arugula in a bowl. Combine vinegar, herbes de Provence, mustard, garlic, ¼ teaspoon salt, and ¼ teaspoon pepper; gradually add 2 tablespoons oil, stirring constantly with a whisk. Drizzle vinaigrette over salad; toss gently to coat.

3 **Heat a skillet** over medium-high heat. Coat pan with cooking spray. Sprinkle chicken with ¼ teaspoon salt and ¼ teaspoon pepper. Add chicken; cook 2 minutes on each side or until done. Divide salad among 4 plates. Cut chicken across grain into thin slices; arrange 1 evenly over salads. Top each with about 2 teaspoons olives. Serves 4

Calories 265; Fat 14.2g (sat 2.1g, mono 9.5g, poly 1.8g); Protein 28g; Carb 6.2g; Fiber 1.8g; Chol 66mg; Iron 1.8mg; Sodium 538mg; Calc 87mg

SIMPLE SWAP *Use turkey, pork, or veal cutlets instead of chicken.*

Chicken *with* Creamy Dijon Sauce

HANDS-ON TIME: 20 min. **TOTAL TIME:** 20 min.

PREP TIP *Pounding the chicken helps shorten cook time, leaving it supremely tender and juicy. The tasty browned bits that remain behind after the chicken cooks become the basis of a speedy sauce.*

4 (6-ounce) skinless, boneless chicken breast halves
¼ teaspoon salt
¼ teaspoon freshly ground black pepper
1 tablespoon olive oil
3 tablespoons chopped shallots

½ cup fat-free, lower-sodium chicken broth
1 rosemary sprig
3 tablespoons whipping cream
2 teaspoons Dijon mustard

1 **Place chicken breast halves** between 2 sheets of plastic wrap; pound to ½-inch thickness. Sprinkle chicken with salt and pepper.

2 **Heat a large skillet** over medium-high heat. Add olive oil to pan. Add chicken; sauté 3 minutes on each side or until done. Transfer to a serving platter.

3 **Add shallots to pan;** sauté 2 minutes. Stir in broth and rosemary sprig; bring to a boil. Cook 2 minutes. Stir in whipping cream; cook 2 minutes, scraping pan to loosen browned bits. Remove from heat, and discard rosemary. Stir in Dijon mustard. Spoon over chicken. Serves 4

SIMPLE SWAP *Use chicken breast cutlets, if you like—you can skip the pounding process.*

Calories 272; Fat 12g (sat 4g, mono 5g, poly 1.2g); Protein 36.7g; Carb 2.3g; Fiber 0.3g; Chol 124mg; Iron 0.8mg; Sodium 518mg; Calc 21mg

SIMPLE SWAP *Use any fresh vegetables you have on hand, such as fresh summer squash, bell peppers, or spinach.*

Chicken *and* Summer Vegetable Tostadas

HANDS-ON TIME: 20 min. **TOTAL TIME:** 20 min.

PREP TIP *A south-of-the-border supper is ready in a snap thanks to quick-cooking chicken tenders. The tostadas can easily become soft tacos if you skip broiling the tortillas. Pair with black beans. Put them on to cook before prepping the tostadas so they'll be warm and ready when the tostadas are finished.*

1 teaspoon ground cumin	1 cup chopped zucchini
¼ teaspoon kosher salt	½ cup salsa verde
¼ teaspoon freshly ground black pepper	3 tablespoons chopped fresh cilantro, divided
2 teaspoons canola oil	4 (8-inch) fat-free flour tortillas
12 ounces chicken breast tenders	Cooking spray
1 cup chopped red onion (about 1)	3 ounces shredded Monterey Jack cheese, (about ¾ cup)
1 cup fresh corn kernels (about 2 ears)	

1 **Preheat broiler.** Combine first 3 ingredients in a small bowl. Heat a large nonstick skillet over medium-high heat. Add oil to pan; swirl to coat. Sprinkle spice mixture evenly over chicken. Add chicken to pan; sauté 3 minutes. Add onion, corn, and zucchini to pan; sauté 2 minutes or until chicken is done. Stir in salsa and 2 tablespoons cilantro. Cook 2 minutes or until liquid almost evaporates, stirring frequently.

2 **Working with 2 tortillas at a time,** arrange tortillas in a single layer on a baking sheet; lightly coat tortillas with cooking spray. Broil 3 minutes or until lightly browned.

3 **Spoon about ¾ cup chicken mixture** in center of each tortilla; sprinkle each serving with about ¼ cup cheese. Broil 2 minutes or until cheese melts. Repeat procedure with remaining tortillas, chicken mixture, and cheese. Sprinkle each serving with about ¾ teaspoon cilantro. Serves 4

Calories 371; Fat 11g (sat 4.6g, mono 3.7g, poly 1.3g); Protein 30.8g; Carb 36.4g; Fiber 3.9g; Chol 68mg; Iron 1.3mg; Sodium 740mg; Calc 182mg

Chicken Tamale
Casserole

HANDS-ON TIME: 10 min. **TOTAL TIME:** 45 min.

This delicious casserole is a quick and easy swap for traditional tamales. Serve it with a mixed green salad and sliced tomatoes, which you can put together while the casserole bakes; toss the salad with a red wine or balsamic vinaigrette.

4 ounces preshredded 4-cheese Mexican blend cheese (about 1 cup), divided

⅓ cup fat-free milk

¼ cup egg substitute

1 teaspoon ground cumin

⅛ teaspoon ground red pepper

1 (14¾-ounce) can cream-style corn

1 (8½-ounce) box corn muffin mix

1 (4-ounce) can chopped green chiles, drained

Cooking spray

1 (10-ounce) can red enchilada sauce

2 cups shredded cooked chicken breast

½ cup fat-free sour cream

1 **Preheat oven to 400°.** Combine ¼ cup cheese and next 7 ingredients (through chiles) in a large bowl, stirring just until moist.

2 **Pour mixture** into a 13 x 9-inch glass or ceramic baking dish coated with cooking spray. Bake at 400° for 15 minutes or until set.

3 **Pierce entire surface liberally** with a fork; pour enchilada sauce over top. Top with chicken; sprinkle with remaining cheese. Bake at 400° for 15 minutes or until cheese melts. Remove from oven; let stand 5 minutes. Cut into 8 pieces; top each serving with 1 tablespoon sour cream. Serves 8

SIMPLE SWAP

Make with shredded cooked turkey instead of chicken, or substitute ground beef or turkey.

Calories 354; Fat 14.1g (sat 7.1g, mono 3.3g, poly 1.2g); Protein 18.9g; Carb 36.3g; Fiber 2.5g; Chol 58mg; Iron 1.7mg; Sodium 620mg; Calc 179mg

Kung Pao Chicken *with* Coconut Jasmine Rice

HANDS-ON TIME: 27 min. **TOTAL TIME:** 27 min.

PREP TIP *This takeout favorite can be prepared at home in less than 30 minutes. Put the rice on to cook after prepping the ingredients for the chicken.*

- 1 cup uncooked jasmine rice
- 2 cups water, divided
- ½ cup light coconut milk
- ¼ teaspoon salt
- ¼ cup chopped fresh cilantro
- 2 tablespoons dark sesame oil
- 1 cup chopped onion
- 2 garlic cloves, minced
- 1 pound skinless, boneless chicken thighs, cut into 1-inch pieces

- 3 tablespoons lower-sodium soy sauce
- 2 teaspoons cornstarch
- 1 to 1½ teaspoons crushed red pepper
- 1 teaspoon brown sugar
- ½ teaspoon bottled minced ginger
- 1 cup thinly sliced red bell pepper (about 1 large pepper)
- 1 cup snow peas, trimmed
- 2 tablespoons chopped unsalted, dry-roasted peanuts

1 **Combine rice,** 1¼ cups water, coconut milk, and salt in a medium saucepan; bring to a boil. Cover and reduce heat to a simmer; cook 15 minutes or until liquid is absorbed and rice is tender. Remove rice from heat; fluff with a fork. Stir in cilantro.

2 **While rice cooks,** heat a large skillet over medium-high heat. Add oil to pan; swirl to coat. Add onion to pan; sauté 3 minutes or until softened. Add garlic; sauté 30 seconds, stirring constantly. Add chicken; sauté 3 minutes or until chicken begins to brown.

3 **Combine ¾ cup water,** soy sauce, and next 4 ingredients (through ginger), stirring until sugar dissolves. Add water mixture to pan; bring to a boil. Add bell pepper and snow peas; cook 2 minutes or until vegetables are crisp-tender and sauce thickens. Sprinkle with nuts; serve with rice. Serves 4 (serving size: 1 cup chicken mixture and ½ cup rice)

Calories 454; Fat 15.3g (sat 3.7g, mono 5.4g, poly 4.8g); Protein 28.3g; Carb 49.4g; Fiber 3.4g; Chol 94mg; Iron 2.4mg; Sodium 657mg; Calc 61mg

SIMPLE SWAP *Make with pork tenderloin instead of chicken thighs.*

Chicken Yakitori Rice Bowl

HANDS-ON TIME: 20 min. **TOTAL TIME:** 20 min.

PREP TIP *Mirin is a rice wine low in alcohol, and most of it cooks off in this recipe. For a nonalcoholic substitute, use a mixture of equal parts rice vinegar and sugar.*

2 (3.5-ounce) bags boil-in-bag basmati rice

¼ cup lower-sodium soy sauce

¼ cup mirin (sweet rice wine)

3 tablespoons sugar

2 tablespoons fat-free, lower-sodium chicken broth

1 tablespoon rice vinegar

3 teaspoons peanut oil, divided

1 pound skinless, boneless chicken thighs

8 ounces snow peas, halved lengthwise diagonally

1 bunch green onions, cut into 1-inch pieces

1 Cook rice according to package directions, omitting salt and fat.

2 While rice cooks, combine soy sauce and next 4 ingredients (through vinegar) in a small saucepan; bring to a boil. Reduce heat; simmer 3 minutes. Remove from heat. Heat a large nonstick skillet or wok over medium-high heat. Add 2 teaspoons oil to pan; swirl to coat. Add chicken thighs to pan; cook 3 minutes on each side or until browned. Transfer to a cutting board; cool slightly. Cut into 1-inch strips.

3 Return pan to medium-high heat; add 1 teaspoon oil to pan. Add snow peas and onions; sauté 2 minutes. Add soy sauce mixture and chicken to pan; cook 2 minutes or until liquid is syrupy and chicken is thoroughly heated, stirring frequently. Place 1 cup rice in each of 4 shallow bowls; top each serving with 1 cup chicken mixture. Serves 4

Calories 441; Fat 8g (sat 1.7g, mono 3g, poly 2.3g); Protein 29.4g; Carb 59.9g; Fiber 2.6g; Chol 94mg; Iron 3.2mg; Sodium 511mg; Calc 71mg

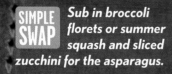

SIMPLE SWAP *Sub in broccoli florets or summer squash and sliced zucchini for the asparagus.*

Spicy-Sweet Chicken Thighs *with* Roasted Asparagus

HANDS-ON TIME: 25 min. **TOTAL TIME:** 25 min.

PREP TIP *This is one of **Cooking Light's** most popular chicken recipes—and for good reason. The sweet heat packs a wallop. For more tender taste buds, cut back on the red pepper. Once the chicken goes in the oven, trim and prep the asparagus on a separate baking sheet, and then place the pan in the oven when you turn the thighs over, cooking until tender.*

2 **teaspoons garlic powder**	8 **skinless, boneless chicken thighs**
2 **teaspoons chili powder**	**Cooking spray**
1 **teaspoon ground cumin**	1 **pound asparagus, trimmed**
1 **teaspoon paprika**	1 **tablespoon olive oil**
½ **teaspoon salt**	6 **tablespoons honey**
½ **teaspoon ground red pepper**	2 **teaspoons cider vinegar**

1 **Preheat broiler.** Combine first 6 ingredients in a large bowl. Add chicken to bowl; toss to coat. Place chicken on a broiler pan coated with cooking spray. Broil chicken 5 minutes on each side.

2 **While chicken cooks, combine asparagus** and oil, tossing to coat. Spread asparagus in a single layer on a baking sheet, and broil 5 minutes or until tender.

3 **While chicken and asparagus cook, combine honey** and vinegar in a bowl, stirring well. Remove chicken from oven; brush ¼ cup honey mixture on chicken. Broil 1 minute. Remove chicken from oven and turn over. Brush chicken with remaining honey mixture. Broil 1 minute or until chicken is done. Serves 4 (serving size: 2 chicken thighs and about 5 asparagus spears)

Calories 363; Fat 14.5g (sat 3.5g, mono 6.6g, poly 2.9g); Protein 29.3g; Carb 30.2g; Fiber 1.8g; Chol 99mg; Iron 3.4mg; Sodium 386mg; Calc 35mg

SIMPLE SWAP Top with cheddar instead of Parmesan. Use cauliflower florets instead of broccoli (or a mix of the two).

Broccoli *and* Rice Casseroles

HANDS-ON TIME: 15 min. **TOTAL TIME:** 40 min.

PREP TIP *To put this together even faster, look for prechopped onions, bell peppers, and celery in the produce section of the supermarket. Serve with steamed carrots. You can also cook this in an 8-inch casserole dish, if you like.*

2 cups 1% low-fat milk
1 cup water
1 (3½-ounce) bag boil-in-bag long-grain rice
3 cups small broccoli florets
Cooking spray
⅓ cup chopped onion
⅓ cup chopped celery
⅓ cup chopped green bell pepper
2 ounces ⅓-less-fat cream cheese (about ¼ cup)

2 ounces light processed cheese, cubed
2 cups shredded skinless, boneless rotisserie chicken breast
¼ teaspoon salt
¼ teaspoon freshly ground black pepper
1 ounce grated fresh Parmesan cheese (about ¼ cup)

1 **Preheat oven to 375°.** Combine milk and 1 cup water in a medium saucepan; bring to a boil. Add rice; cook 10 minutes. Remove rice; keep warm. Return milk mixture to a simmer. Add broccoli; cook 5 minutes. Drain; discard milk mixture.

2 **While broccoli cooks, heat a Dutch oven** over medium-high heat. Coat pan with cooking spray. Add onion, celery, and bell pepper; sauté 5 minutes. Add cream cheese and processed cheese, stirring until cheeses melt. Remove from heat; stir in rice, broccoli, chicken, salt, and black pepper.

3 **Spoon 1 cup rice mixture** into each of 4 (10-ounce) ramekins coated with cooking spray. Sprinkle each serving with 1 tablespoon Parmesan. Bake at 375° for 10 minutes or until cheese melts. Serves 4 (serving size: 1 casserole)

Calories 327; Fat 9.5g (sat 5.2g, mono 2.5g, poly 0.5g); Protein 29g; Carb 31.3g; Fiber 2.2g; Chol 76mg; Iron 1.7mg; Sodium 633mg; Calc 284mg

SIMPLE SWAP

Prepare these lettuce cups using ground turkey, if you like.

Chicken Lettuce Cups

HANDS-ON TIME: 17 min. **TOTAL TIME:** 17 min.

PREP TIP *The artichokes and olives amp up the flavor of this dish. To prep it even faster, toss the herbs, onion, artichokes, tomato, and olives in a food processor and pulse. Serve with orzo with spinach. Start the orzo before you make the lettuce cups. You can stir in fresh spinach at the end. The heat from the orzo will wilt it.*

Cooking spray
1 pound ground chicken
¼ teaspoon freshly ground black pepper
⅛ teaspoon salt
1 cup vertically sliced red onion
½ cup canned artichoke hearts, drained and coarsely chopped
¼ cup diced tomato

1 tablespoon chopped fresh oregano
1 tablespoon chopped fresh flat-leaf parsley
10 pitted green olives, chopped
3 ounces diced fresh mozzarella cheese (about ½ cup)
1 tablespoon fresh lemon juice
8 Bibb lettuce leaves

1 **Heat a large skillet** over medium-high heat. Coat pan with cooking spray. Add chicken, pepper, and salt; cook 3 minutes, stirring to crumble.

2 **Stir in onion** and next 5 ingredients (through olives); cook 3 minutes or until chicken is done.

3 **Stir in cheese and juice.** Spoon 1¼ cups chicken mixture into each lettuce leaf. Serves 4 (serving size: 2 lettuce cups)

Calories 275; Fat 16.9g (sat 5.6g, mono 7g, poly 2.3g); Protein 24.6g; Carb 6.9g; Fiber 0.9g; Chol 115mg; Iron 1.6mg; Sodium 495mg; Calc 27mg

SIMPLE SWAP ***Change up the flavor of this dish by using any variety of chicken or turkey sausages that you like.***

Polenta *and* Spicy Sauce Sausage

HANDS-ON TIME: 25 min. **TOTAL TIME:** 39 min.

 PREP TIP *Crushed red pepper adds a kick, but you can decrease the amount to cool this dish down. Pair this with a side of sautéed spinach topped with toasted pine nuts. You can prepare it as soon as you stir the cheese into the polenta in step 3. Remove the polenta from the heat and cover. The side will take just minutes to prepare.*

1 tablespoon olive oil
6 ounces sun-dried tomato chicken sausage (2 links), sliced
1 cup chopped onion
3 garlic cloves, minced
1 tablespoon chopped fresh oregano
½ teaspoon crushed red pepper
2 (14½-ounce) cans unsalted diced tomatoes, undrained

½ cup chopped fresh basil, divided
2 cups fat-free, lower-sodium chicken broth
1 cup water
¾ cup quick-cooking polenta
2 ounces grated fresh Parmesan cheese (about ½ cup), divided

1 **Heat a medium saucepan** over medium-high heat. Add oil to pan; swirl to coat. Add sausage; sauté 3 minutes or until browned.

2 **Add onion;** sauté 5 minutes or until tender. Add garlic; sauté 30 seconds. Add oregano, pepper, and tomatoes; bring to a boil. Reduce heat, and simmer 15 minutes, stirring occasionally. Add ¼ cup basil to pan; cook 5 minutes or until sauce thickens.

3 **While sauce cooks, combine broth** and 1 cup water in a large saucepan; bring to a boil. Add polenta; reduce heat, and simmer 5 minutes or until thick, stirring frequently with a whisk. Stir in half of cheese. Place ⅔ cup polenta in each of 4 bowls; top with about ¾ cup sauce. Top each serving with 1 tablespoon basil and 1 tablespoon cheese. Serves 4

Calories 311; Fat 10g (sat 3.2g, mono 4.8g, poly 1.5g); Protein 16.4g; Carb 31.5g; Fiber 5.3g; Chol 41.3mg; Iron 1.8mg; Sodium 644mg; Calc 170mg

Sausage-Spinach Rice Bowl

HANDS-ON TIME: 10 min. **TOTAL TIME:** 10 min.

PREP TIP *Serve this hearty rice bowl with Garlicky Asparagus on page 197. To make sure everything is ready at once, prep all your ingredients before starting. While the rice heats, you can make the asparagus and the sausage and spinach mixture in two pans at the same time.*

1 (8.8-ounce) pouch precooked brown rice

1 tablespoon olive oil

6 ounces hot turkey Italian sausage, casings removed

⅛ teaspoon crushed red pepper

5 garlic cloves, thinly sliced

1 (6-ounce) package fresh baby spinach

1 ounce fresh Parmigiano-Reggiano cheese, shaved (about ¼ cup)

1 **Heat rice** according to package directions.

2 **While rice heats, heat a large skillet** over medium-high heat. Add oil to pan; swirl to coat. Add sausage and pepper; cook 4 minutes or until sausage is browned, stirring to crumble. Add garlic; cook 30 seconds, stirring constantly. Add spinach; cook 30 seconds or until spinach begins to wilt, tossing constantly.

3 **Stir in rice;** cook 1 minute or until heated. Sprinkle with cheese. Serves 3 (serving size: 1 cup)

SIMPLE SWAP *Vary this dish by using different types of greens. Sub in kale, Swiss chard, or arugula for the spinach.*

Calories 333; Fat 15.4g (sat 4.3g, mono 7g, poly 3.6g); Protein 17.5g; Carb 33g; Fiber 4g; Chol 40mg; Iron 3.4mg; Sodium 610mg; Calc 161mg

Sautéed Turkey Cutlets *with* Orange-Cranberry Sauce

HANDS-ON TIME: 20 min. **TOTAL TIME:** 20 min.

 PREP TIP *Turkey cutlets cook in a flash, taking just minutes to prepare. Serve with a wild rice mix, which you should start before you cook the cutlets.*

- 8 (2-ounce) turkey cutlets
- ¼ teaspoon salt
- ¼ teaspoon freshly ground black pepper
- ¼ cup all-purpose flour
- 1 tablespoon butter
- 1 tablespoon canola oil
- 1 cup fresh orange juice
- ⅓ cup dried cranberries
- 2 teaspoons Dijon mustard

1 **Sprinkle cutlets** with salt and pepper. Place flour in a shallow dish. Dredge cutlets in flour; shake off excess flour.

2 **Melt butter** and oil in a large nonstick skillet over low heat. Increase heat to medium-high; heat 2 minutes or until butter turns golden brown. Add cutlets to pan; cook 2 minutes on each side or until golden brown. Remove cutlets from pan; keep warm.

3 **Add juice,** cranberries, and mustard to pan, scraping pan to loosen browned bits. Bring to a boil; cook 5 minutes or until reduced to ⅔ cup. Serve sauce over cutlets. Serves 4 (serving size: 2 cutlets and about 2½ tablespoons sauce)

 SIMPLE SWAP *Make with skinless, boneless chicken breast cutlets instead of turkey.*

Calories 260; Fat 7.2g (sat 2.3g, mono 3.1g, poly 1.4g); Protein 29.1g; Carb 19.8g; Fiber 0.9g; Chol 53mg; Iron 1.9mg; Sodium 332mg; Calc 10mg

SIMPLE SWAP *Substitute 1 (1-pound) flank steak for the tenderloin, or use boneless center-cut loin pork chops instead. You may need to decrease the cook time depending on the thickness of the chops.*

Beef Tenderloin Steaks *with* Balsamic Green Beans *and* Parmesan Potatoes

HANDS-ON TIME: 35 min. **TOTAL TIME:** 35 min.

PREP TIP *Beef tenderloin is a lean cut that doesn't require much time over the heat, making it a delicious option for weeknight meals.*

- 2 teaspoons butter, divided
- 1 cup vertically sliced yellow onion
- 1 cup vertically sliced red onion
- ¼ cup sliced shallots
- 3 garlic cloves, minced
- ½ cup fat-free, lower-sodium beef broth
- 2 cups green beans, trimmed
- 2 tablespoons balsamic vinegar
- ¼ teaspoon salt, divided
- 4 (4-ounce) beef tenderloin steaks
- ⅜ teaspoon freshly ground black pepper, divided
- Cooking spray
- 2 cups refrigerated mashed potatoes
- 2 ounces grated fresh Parmesan cheese (about ½ cup)
- ¼ cup thinly sliced green onions

1 **Melt 1 teaspoon butter** in a saucepan over medium-high heat. Add yellow onion, red onion, and shallots; sauté 6 minutes. Add garlic; sauté 1 minute. Add broth; cook 4 minutes or until onion is tender. Add beans and vinegar; cover and cook 4 minutes or until beans are crisp-tender. Remove from heat. Stir in 1 teaspoon butter and ⅛ teaspoon salt; keep warm.

2 **Sprinkle steaks** with ⅛ teaspoon salt and ¼ teaspoon pepper. Heat a cast-iron skillet over medium-high heat. Coat pan with cooking spray. Add steaks to pan; cook 3 minutes on each side or until desired degree of doneness. Let stand 5 minutes.

3 **While steaks stand, heat a saucepan** over medium heat. Add potatoes; cover and cook 5 minutes or until thoroughly heated, stirring occasionally. Stir in cheese, green onions, and ⅛ teaspoon pepper. Serves 4 (serving size: 1 steak, ½ cup bean mixture, and about ½ cup potatoes)

Calories 408; Fat 17g (sat 9g, mono 4.7g, poly 0.6g); Protein 34.6g; Carb 29.5g; Fiber 5.4g; Chol 103mg; Iron 3.3mg; Sodium 694mg; Calc 264mg

Barbecue Sirloin *and* Blue Cheese Salad

HANDS-ON TIME: 22 min. **TOTAL TIME:** 26 min.

 PREP TIP *Allow the steak to rest after cooking so the juices redistribute, keeping the meat juicy.*

- 2 teaspoons chili powder
- ¾ teaspoon ground cumin
- ½ teaspoon garlic powder
- ¼ teaspoon salt, divided
- ¼ teaspoon freshly ground black pepper, divided
- 1 pound lean sirloin steak, trimmed
- Cooking spray
- 2 tablespoons white wine vinegar

- 2 teaspoons Dijon mustard
- 1 tablespoon extra-virgin olive oil
- 6 cups torn Bibb lettuce
- 1 cup red bell pepper strips
- ¾ cup thinly sliced peeled cucumber
- ½ cup thinly sliced shallots
- 2 ounces crumbled blue cheese (about ½ cup)

 Combine chili powder, cumin, garlic powder, ⅛ teaspoon salt, and ⅛ teaspoon black pepper; rub evenly over both sides of steak.

Heat a grill pan over medium-high heat. Coat pan with cooking spray. Add steak to pan; cook 5 minutes. Turn steak over; cook 4 minutes or until desired degree of doneness. Place steak on a cutting board; let stand 5 minutes. Cut across grain into thin slices.

While steak stands, combine vinegar, mustard, ⅛ teaspoon salt, and ⅛ teaspoon black pepper in a bowl. Gradually add oil, stirring with a whisk. Combine lettuce, bell pepper, cucumber, and shallots in a bowl. Drizzle vinaigrette over salad; toss gently. Top salad with steak and cheese. Serves 4 (serving size: about 1½ cups salad, 3 ounces steak, and 2 tablespoons cheese)

Calories 269; Fat 12.4g (sat 4.9g, mono 5.4g, poly 0.8g); Protein 29.5g; Carb 9.4g; Fiber 2.6g; Chol 57mg; Iron 2.8mg; Sodium 526mg; Calc 141mg

 SIMPLE SWAP *Make with grilled pork tenderloin instead of beef sirloin.*

Herb-Roasted Beef *and* Potatoes

HANDS-ON TIME: 25 min. **TOTAL TIME:** 45 min.

PREP TIP *Serve with roasted Brussels sprouts, asparagus, or broccoli. You can cook them until they're deliciously browned and tender in the oven alongside the meat and potatoes for an easy, virtually hands-off meal.*

- 2 **tablespoons chopped fresh thyme, divided**
- 1 **tablespoon chopped fresh rosemary**
- 1 **tablespoon chopped fresh parsley**
- 2½ **tablespoons olive oil, divided**
- 1 **teaspoon kosher salt, divided**
- ¾ **teaspoon freshly ground black pepper, divided**
- 2 **garlic cloves, minced**
- 2 **(8-ounce) beef shoulder tender roasts, trimmed**
- **Cooking spray**
- 1 **(20-ounce) package refrigerated potato wedges**

1 **Preheat broiler.** Combine 1 tablespoon thyme, rosemary, parsley, 1 tablespoon oil, ½ teaspoon salt, ½ teaspoon pepper, and garlic; rub evenly over both sides of beef. Coat rack of a broiler pan with cooking spray. Place beef on rack; place rack in pan.

2 **Combine potatoes,** 1½ tablespoons oil, ½ teaspoon salt, and ¼ teaspoon pepper. Arrange potato mixture on rack around beef. Broil 7 minutes. Turn beef over. Broil 7 minutes or until beef is desired degree of doneness. Remove from oven. Place beef on a cutting board; let stand 5 minutes.

3 **Stir potatoes;** sprinkle with 1 tablespoon thyme. Cut beef across grain into thin slices; serve with potatoes. Serves 4 (serving size: 3 ounces beef and ¾ cup potatoes)

SIMPLE SWAP *If you can't find shoulder tender roast, use beef or pork tenderloin.*

Calories 318; Fat 14.6g (sat 3.6g, mono 8.7g, poly 1.3g); Protein 26.1g; Carb 18.7g; Fiber 3.9g; Chol 66mg; Iron 3.2mg; Sodium 668mg; Calc 16mg

SIMPLE SWAP

You can also make this with grilled chicken or lamb.

Thai Steak Salad

HANDS-ON TIME: 23 min. **TOTAL TIME:** 35 min.

 PREP TIP *Put this salad together even faster by using packaged julienne-cut carrots.*

Cooking spray
1 (1½-pound) flank steak, trimmed
½ teaspoon freshly ground black pepper
⅛ teaspoon kosher salt
¼ cup fresh lime juice
1 tablespoon brown sugar
2 tablespoons lower-sodium soy sauce
1 tablespoon fish sauce

2 teaspoons minced fresh garlic
1 teaspoon Sriracha (hot chile sauce)
1½ cups thinly sliced napa (Chinese) cabbage
1¼ cups fresh bean sprouts
¾ cup julienne-cut carrots
⅓ cup mint leaves
⅓ cup cilantro leaves
⅓ cup basil leaves

1 **Heat a large grill pan** over medium-high heat. Coat pan with cooking spray. Sprinkle steak evenly with pepper and salt. Add steak to pan; cook 6 minutes on each side or until desired degree of doneness. Remove steak from pan; let stand 5 minutes. Cut steak diagonally across grain into thin slices.

2 **While steak stands, combine juice** and next 5 ingredients (through Sriracha) in a small bowl; stir with a whisk.

3 **Combine cabbage** and remaining ingredients in a medium bowl. Add 6 tablespoons juice mixture to cabbage mixture; toss well. Toss steak in remaining juice mixture. Add steak to cabbage mixture; toss to combine. Serves 4 (serving size: about 4 ounces steak and 1 cup salad)

Calories 297; Fat 9.8g (sat 3.6g, mono 3.3g, poly 0.5g); Protein 39.5g; Carb 12.6g; Fiber 2.3g; Chol 56mg; Iron 3.6mg; Sodium 687mg; Calc 86mg

Cheesy Meat Loaf Minis

HANDS-ON TIME: 15 min. **TOTAL TIME:** 40 min.

PREP TIP *This will become your go-to weeknight meat loaf recipe. The horseradish adds a welcome, pungent kick. Serve with a simple salad made with 1 (5-ounce) package of herb salad mix, carrot ribbons, and sliced red onion and drizzled with balsamic vinaigrette. It will be an easy side to toss together while the meat loaves cook.*

1 ounce fresh breadcrumbs (about ½ cup)
Cooking spray
1 cup chopped onion
2 garlic cloves, chopped
½ cup ketchup, divided
¼ cup chopped fresh parsley
2 tablespoons grated fresh Parmesan cheese
1 tablespoon prepared horseradish
1 tablespoon Dijon mustard
¾ teaspoon dried oregano
¼ teaspoon salt
¼ teaspoon freshly ground black pepper
3 ounces white cheddar cheese (about ¾ cup), diced
1½ pounds ground sirloin
1 large egg, lightly beaten

 Preheat oven to 425°. Heat a small skillet over medium-high heat. Add breadcrumbs; cook 3 minutes or until toasted, stirring frequently.

 While breadcrumbs cook, heat a large skillet over medium-high heat. Coat pan with cooking spray. Add onion and garlic, and sauté 3 minutes.

 Combine onion mixture, breadcrumbs, ¼ cup ketchup, and next 10 ingredients (through egg). Shape into 6 (4 x 2-inch) loaves on a broiler pan coated with cooking spray; spread 2 teaspoons ketchup over each. Bake at 425° for 25 minutes or until done. Serves 6 (serving size: 1 meat loaf)

Calories 254; Fat 11.4g (sat 5.6g, mono 3.8g, poly 0.9g); Protein 28.3g; Carb 11.1g; Fiber 0.9g; Chol 112mg; Iron 2.6mg; Sodium 607mg; Calc 150mg

Pork *with* Pomegranate Sauce *and* Sour Cream Mashed Potatoes

HANDS-ON TIME: 20 min. **TOTAL TIME:** 20 min.

PREP TIP

This is elegant enough for a dinner party, but easy enough for a weeknight dinner. Pair it with steamed or sautéed green beans, kale, or spinach.

- ½ teaspoon garlic powder
- ½ teaspoon salt
- ½ teaspoon ground cumin
- ½ teaspoon freshly ground black pepper, divided
- 4 (4-ounce) boneless center-cut loin pork chops
- 2 teaspoons olive oil
- ⅓ cup chopped shallots
- ¾ cup pomegranate juice
- 1 tablespoon sugar
- 1 tablespoon balsamic vinegar
- 2 cups refrigerated mashed potatoes
- ⅓ cup reduced-fat sour cream
- 1 tablespoon minced fresh chives

1 **Combine garlic powder,** salt, cumin, and ¼ teaspoon pepper in a small bowl; sprinkle evenly over pork chops.

2 **Heat a nonstick skillet** over medium-high heat. Add oil to pan; swirl to coat. Add pork chops; cook 3 minutes on each side or until done. Remove and keep warm. Add shallots to pan; cook 45 seconds, stirring constantly. Add juice, sugar, and vinegar; bring to a boil. Cook 5 minutes or until slightly thick.

3 **While sauce cooks, heat a small saucepan** over medium heat. Add mashed potatoes; cover and cook 5 minutes or until thoroughly heated, stirring occasionally. Stir in sour cream and ¼ teaspoon pepper. Top with chives. Serves 4 (serving size: 1 pork chop, about 2 tablespoons sauce, and about ½ cup mashed potatoes)

Calories 364; Fat 14.8g (sat 6.8g, mono 5.3g, poly 0.9g); Protein 27g; Carb 30.6g; Fiber 2.4g; Chol 87mg; Iron 2mg; Sodium 554mg; Calc 93mg

SIMPLE SWAP *Make with skinless, boneless chicken breasts instead of pork chops.*

Coconut Curried Pork, Snow Pea, *and* Mango Stir-Fry

HANDS-ON TIME: 15 min. **TOTAL TIME:** 15 min.

PREP TIP *Red curry powder is a blend of coriander, cumin, chiles, and cardamom; use it to give any dish a hit of Thai flavor. If you like, serve this with an arugula salad dressed with a lime juice vinaigrette. Prep all the ingredients before you begin the stir-fry.*

- 2 (3½-ounce) bags boil-in-bag long-grain rice
- 1 tablespoon canola oil
- 1 (1-pound) pork tenderloin, trimmed and cut into 1-inch cubes
- 1 teaspoon red curry powder
- 1 cup snow peas, trimmed
- ⅓ cup light coconut milk

- 1 tablespoon fish sauce
- 1 teaspoon red curry paste
- 1 cup bottled mango, cut into ½-inch pieces
- ½ cup sliced green onions, divided
- 2 tablespoons shredded coconut
- 4 lime wedges (optional)

 Cook rice according to package directions, omitting salt and fat; drain.

 While rice cooks, heat a large nonstick skillet over medium-high heat. Add oil to pan; swirl to coat. Sprinkle pork evenly with curry powder. Add pork and snow peas to pan; stir-fry 3 minutes.

3 Combine coconut milk, fish sauce, and curry paste. Add milk mixture to pan; bring to a simmer. Stir in mango and ¼ cup onions; cook 1 minute or until heated. Remove from heat. Place 1 cup rice on each of 4 plates; top each with 1¼ cups pork mixture. Sprinkle each with 1 tablespoon green onions and 1½ teaspoons shredded coconut. Serve with lime wedges, if desired. Serves 4

Calories 429; Fat 9.7g (sat 3.5g, mono 3.9g, poly 1.6g); Protein 29.7g; Carb 54.8g; Fiber 2.3g; Chol 74mg; Iron 4mg; Sodium 454mg; Calc 38mg

SIMPLE SWAP *Use any variety of tomato you like. Choose a mix of heirloom tomatoes to make this dish extra colorful.*

Pork *and* Tomato Skillet Sauté

HANDS-ON TIME: 25 min. **TOTAL TIME:** 25 min.

 PREP TIP *Add a couple large handfuls of fresh spinach to the skillet and cook alongside the pork and tomatoes until wilted for an easy side dish.*

- 4 teaspoons olive oil, divided
- 4 (6-ounce) bone-in center-cut loin pork chops, trimmed (about ½ inch thick)
- ½ teaspoon salt, divided
- ½ teaspoon freshly ground black pepper, divided
- ½ cup thinly sliced shallots
- 2 tablespoons balsamic vinegar
- 2 teaspoons minced fresh garlic
- 2 cups grape tomatoes
- 3 tablespoons fresh basil leaves

1 **Heat a large nonstick skillet** over medium-high heat. Add 1 teaspoon oil to pan; swirl to coat. Sprinkle chops evenly with ¼ teaspoon salt and ¼ teaspoon pepper. Add pork to pan; cook 3 minutes on each side or until done. Remove pork from pan.

2 **Add 1 tablespoon oil,** shallots, vinegar, and garlic to pan; sauté 1 minute, scraping pan to loosen browned bits.

3 **Combine tomatoes,** ¼ teaspoon salt, and ¼ teaspoon pepper in a medium bowl; toss gently to coat. Add tomato mixture to pan; cook 2 minutes or until tomatoes begin to soften. Sprinkle with basil. Serve tomato mixture with pork. Serves 4 (serving size: 1 chop and about ½ cup tomato mixture)

Calories 255; Fat 10.7g (sat 2.4g, mono 5.5g, poly 1.2g); Protein 25.3g; Carb 15.1g; Fiber 1.1g; Chol 71mg; Iron 1.6mg; Sodium 348mg; Calc 41mg

Pork Chops *with* Roasted Apples *and* Onions

HANDS-ON TIME: 25 min. **TOTAL TIME:** 25 min.

 PREP TIP *Serve with steamed green beans. Two 8-ounce packages of microwave steam-in-bag green beans will produce an almost-effortless side.*

2½ teaspoons canola oil, divided

1½ cups frozen pearl onions, thawed

2 cups Gala apple wedges

1 tablespoon butter, divided

2 teaspoons thyme leaves

½ teaspoon kosher salt, divided

½ teaspoon freshly ground black pepper, divided

4 (6-ounce) bone-in center-cut loin pork chops (about ½ inch thick)

½ cup fat-free, lower-sodium chicken broth

½ teaspoon all-purpose flour

1 teaspoon cider vinegar

1 **Preheat oven to 400°.** Heat a large oven-proof skillet over medium-high heat. Add 1 teaspoon oil to pan; swirl to coat. Pat onions dry and add to pan; cook 2 minutes or until lightly browned, stirring once. Add apples to pan; place in oven. Bake at 400° for 10 minutes or until onions and apples are tender. Stir in 2 teaspoons butter, thyme, ¼ teaspoon salt, and ¼ teaspoon pepper.

2 **While onions and apples cook, heat a large skillet** over medium-high heat. Sprinkle pork with ¼ teaspoon salt and ¼ teaspoon pepper. Add 1½ teaspoons oil to pan; swirl to coat. Add pork; cook 3 minutes on each side or until done. Remove pork from pan; keep warm.

3 **Combine broth and flour** in a small bowl, stirring with a whisk. Add broth mixture to pan; bring to a boil, scraping pan to loosen browned bits. Cook 1 minute or until reduced to ¼ cup. Stir in vinegar and 1 teaspoon butter. Serves 4 (serving size: 1 chop, about 1 tablespoon sauce, and ¾ cup apple mixture)

Calories 240; Fat 10g (sat 3.3g, mono 4.1g, poly 1.4g); Protein 24.9g; Carb 11g; Fiber 1.5g; Chol 84mg; Iron 1mg; Sodium 379mg; Calc 28mg

Szechuan Green Beans *with* Ground Pork

HANDS-ON TIME: 15 min. **TOTAL TIME:** 15 min.

PREP TIP *This hearty, filling meal has a bit of a kick from the crushed red pepper. You can reduce it if you'd prefer a milder dish.*

- 1 cup uncooked white rice
- ½ pound lean ground pork
- 1 teaspoon cornstarch
- ⅛ teaspoon salt
- ⅛ teaspoon freshly ground white pepper
- 1 teaspoon peanut oil
- 2½ cups (1-inch) cut green beans
- 1 teaspoon minced fresh garlic
- 2 tablespoons hoisin sauce
- 1 teaspoon sugar
- 1 teaspoon crushed red pepper
- 2 teaspoons lower-sodium soy sauce

1 **Cook rice** according to package directions, omitting salt and fat.

2 **While rice cooks, combine pork** and next 3 ingredients (through white pepper) in a medium bowl. Heat a large nonstick skillet over medium-high heat. Add oil to pan; swirl to coat. Add pork mixture, beans, and garlic; cook 3 minutes or until pork loses its pink color, stirring to crumble.

3 **Combine hoisin** and next 3 ingredients (through soy sauce) in a small bowl, stirring with a whisk. Add hoisin mixture to pan. Cook 2 minutes or until thoroughly heated, stirring frequently. Serves 4 (serving size: 1 cup pork mixture and ½ cup rice)

SIMPLE SWAP *Substitute lean ground chicken or turkey instead of pork and snow peas in place of green beans.*

Calories 254; Fat 6.8g (sat 2.2g, mono 3.5g, poly 1.1g); Protein 14.6g; Carb 32.5g; Fiber 3.3g; Chol 43mg; Iron 1.5mg; Sodium 323mg; Calc 47mg

Greek Lamb Chops *with* Mint-Yogurt Sauce *and* Tomato-Parsley Salad

HANDS-ON TIME: 30 min. **TOTAL TIME:** 30 min.

 PREP TIP *This dish is simply stunning—and quick. Let the lamb stand at room temperature for 30 minutes so it cooks evenly and quickly.*

- ¼ cup plus ½ teaspoon fresh lemon juice, divided
- 1½ teaspoons Dijon mustard
- ½ teaspoon honey
- 1 tablespoon extra-virgin olive oil
- 2 cups flat-leaf parsley leaves
- 1 cup diced yellow bell pepper
- ½ cup diced red onion
- 1 pint grape tomatoes, halved
- 2 teaspoons chopped fresh oregano
- 3 garlic cloves, minced and divided
- 8 (4-ounce) lamb loin chops, trimmed
- ³/₈ teaspoon kosher salt, divided
- ¼ teaspoon black pepper
- 2 teaspoons canola oil
- ½ cup plain fat-free yogurt
- 1 tablespoon chopped fresh mint

1 **Combine 2 tablespoons lemon juice,** Dijon mustard, and honey in a large bowl; gradually stir in olive oil. Add parsley, bell pepper, onion, and tomatoes; toss gently to coat.

2 **Combine 2 tablespoons lemon juice,** oregano, and 2 garlic cloves. Sprinkle lamb with ¼ teaspoon salt and black pepper; rub with oregano mixture. Heat a skillet over high heat. Add canola oil to pan; swirl to coat. Add lamb; cook 3 minutes on each side or until desired degree of doneness. Let stand 5 minutes.

3 **While chops stand, combine yogurt,** mint, ½ teaspoon lemon juice, ⅛ teaspoon salt, and 1 garlic clove in a small bowl. Serve sauce with lamb. Serves 4 (serving size: 2 lamb chops, 2 tablespoons sauce, and about 1 cup salad)

Calories 429; Fat 18g (sat 5.5g, mono 9g, poly 1.7g); Protein 50.2g; Carb 14.6g; Fiber 3.2g; Chol 147mg; Iron 6.6mg; Sodium 415mg; Calc 148mg

 SIMPLE SWAP *Use mixed greens in place of parsley in the salad and sub Greek yogurt to make a thicker sauce.*

Moroccan-Style Lamb *with* Couscous-Arugula Salad

HANDS-ON TIME: 20 min. **TOTAL TIME:** 20 min.

PREP TIP *Sautéing the spices briefly with the veggies allows their flavors to bloom.*

- 1 cup water
- ¾ cup uncooked couscous
- 2 cups arugula
- 2 tablespoons fresh lemon juice, divided
- 1 pound lean ground lamb
- 2 teaspoons extra-virgin olive oil
- 2 cups vertically sliced onion
- ½ cup (¼-inch) diagonally cut carrot
- ¾ teaspoon ground cumin
- ¾ teaspoon ground cinnamon
- ½ teaspoon ground coriander
- ¼ teaspoon ground red pepper
- 2 cups fat-free, lower-sodium chicken broth
- ½ cup golden raisins
- 3 tablespoons tomato paste
- 1½ tablespoons grated lemon rind
- 1 (15½-ounce) can chickpeas (garbanzo beans), rinsed and drained
- ½ cup chopped fresh cilantro

1 **Bring 1 cup water to a boil** in a medium saucepan. Stir in couscous. Remove from heat; cover and let stand 10 minutes. Fluff couscous with a fork. Stir in arugula and 1 tablespoon lemon juice.

2 **While couscous stands, heat a large nonstick skillet** over medium-high heat. Add lamb to pan; cook 6 minutes, stirring to crumble. Remove lamb from pan with a slotted spoon. Discard drippings.

3 **Add oil to pan;** swirl to coat. Add onion and carrot; sauté 4 minutes. Add cumin, cinnamon, coriander, and pepper; sauté 30 seconds. Add lamb, broth, and next 4 ingredients; bring to a boil. Reduce heat; simmer 4 minutes or until mixture thickens. Remove from heat. Stir in cilantro and 1 tablespoon lemon juice. Serves 4 (serving size: 1¼ cups lamb mixture and about ½ cup couscous)

Calories 552; Fat 20.7g (sat 7.4g, mono 8.8g, poly 1.7g); Protein 30.9g; Carb 61.8g; Fiber 7.8g; Chol 83mg; Iron 3.9mg; Sodium 719mg; Calc 110mg

3

seafood»

Fish and shellfish are
a dream for the busy
weeknight cook–they're
lean and cook quickly.

Arctic Char *with* Orange-Caper Relish

HANDS-ON TIME: 25 min. **TOTAL TIME:** 25 min.

 PREP TIP *You can prepare the relish up to a day in advance. Pair with Frisée and Arugula Salad on page 192. You can prep it while the fish cooks.*

- 1 cup orange sections
- 2 tablespoons slivered red onion
- 1 tablespoon chopped fresh flat-leaf parsley
- 1 tablespoon capers, minced
- 1 teaspoon grated orange rind
- 1 tablespoon fresh orange juice
- 1 tablespoon extra-virgin olive oil
- 1 teaspoon rice vinegar
- ⅛ teaspoon ground red pepper
- 4 (6-ounce) arctic char fillets
- ½ teaspoon kosher salt
- ½ teaspoon freshly ground black pepper
- Cooking spray

1 **Combine first 9 ingredients** in a small bowl. Cover and chill until ready to serve.

 2 **Heat a large heavy skillet** over medium-high heat. Sprinkle fish with salt and black pepper. Coat pan with cooking spray.

 3 **Add fish to pan;** cook 4 minutes on each side or until fish flakes easily when tested with a fork or until desired degree of doneness. Serves 4 (serving size: 1 fillet and about ¼ cup relish)

Calories 295; Fat 18.5g (sat 2.9g, mono 7.7g, poly 2.4g); Protein 26.5g; Carb 6.7g; Fiber 1.4g; Chol 78mg; Iron 1.3mg; Sodium 366mg; Calc 77mg

If you can't find pancetta, substitute prosciutto or unsmoked bacon.

64

Striped Bass All'amatriciana

HANDS-ON TIME: 16 min. **TOTAL TIME:** 23 min.

 PREP TIP *Serve with a simple salad of arugula and thinly sliced fennel bulb tossed with a light vinaigrette and topped with shaved Parmesan for a salty finish. You can prepare the salad while the fish cooks.*

- 3 teaspoons extra-virgin olive oil, divided
- 4 (6-ounce) striped bass fillets
- 3/8 teaspoon salt, divided
- 2 ounces pancetta, finely chopped
- 1/2 cup chopped onion
- 1/8 teaspoon crushed red pepper
- 3 garlic cloves, minced
- 2 cups cherry tomatoes, quartered
- 1 teaspoon balsamic vinegar

1 **Heat a large nonstick skillet** over medium-high heat. Add 2 teaspoons oil to pan; swirl to coat. Sprinkle fish with 1/4 teaspoon salt. Add fish to pan, skin sides up; cook 3 minutes or until lightly browned.

 2 **Turn fish over;** cook 4 minutes or until fish flakes easily when tested with a fork. Remove fish from pan; keep warm.

 3 **Return pan to medium-high heat.** Add 1 teaspoon oil and pancetta; cook 1 minute, stirring occasionally. Add onion, red pepper, and garlic; cook 5 minutes or until pancetta is browned, stirring occasionally. Add tomatoes and vinegar; cook 3 minutes or until tomatoes soften, stirring frequently. Add 1/8 teaspoon salt, stirring well. Spoon sauce over fish. Serves 4 (serving size: 1 fillet and 1/4 cup sauce)

Calories 272; Fat 12.1g (sat 3.4g, mono 5.4g, poly 2.1g); Protein 33.2g; Carb 5.8g; Fiber 1.3g; Chol 146mg; Iron 1.7mg; Sodium 577mg; Calc 42mg

Chip-Crusted Fish Fillets

HANDS-ON TIME: 5 min. **TOTAL TIME:** 15 min.

 The tang in the salt and vinegar chips mellows as the fish bakes. Crush the chips in the bag for less mess. Pair this crunchy spin on fish and chips with a simple side salad, which can be tossed together while the fish is in the oven.

4 (6-ounce) cod fillets
2 teaspoons canola mayonnaise
⅛ teaspoon salt

1 (2-ounce) package salt and vinegar kettle-style potato chips, crushed
½ cup light ranch dressing

1 **Preheat oven to 400°.** Line a baking sheet with parchment paper.

2 **Arrange fish** on prepared baking sheet. Brush ½ teaspoon mayonnaise over top of each fillet; sprinkle evenly with salt. Gently press about 2 tablespoons crushed chips evenly on top of each fillet.

3 **Bake at 400°** for 10 minutes or until fish flakes easily when tested with a fork. Serve with ranch dressing. Serves 4 (serving size: 1 fillet and 2 tablespoons dressing)

Calories 291; Fat 11.3g (sat 1.2g, mono 5.7g, poly 2.8g); Protein 31.7g; Carb 14.5g; Fiber 0.8g; Chol 79mg; Iron 1.4mg; Sodium 549mg; Calc 49mg

Jerk-Rubbed Catfish *with* Spicy Cilantro Slaw

HANDS-ON TIME: 13 min. **TOTAL TIME:** 13 min.

PREP TIP *For maximum heat, leave the seeds and membranes in the chile pepper. Warning: Habanero peppers will be much hotter than serranos. Wear gloves to avoid burning your hands while you chop them.*

- 3 cups packaged cabbage-and-carrot coleslaw
- 2 tablespoons chopped fresh cilantro
- 3 tablespoons canola mayonnaise
- 2 tablespoons fresh lime juice
- 1½ teaspoons sugar
- 1 to 1½ teaspoons finely chopped habanero or serrano pepper
- Cooking spray
- 4 (6-ounce) catfish fillets
- 4 teaspoons Jamaican jerk seasoning

1 **Combine first 6 ingredients** in a medium bowl; toss well to coat.

2 **Heat a grill pan** over medium-high heat. Coat pan with cooking spray. Sprinkle fish evenly with jerk seasoning.

3 **Add fish to pan;** cook 3 minutes on each side or until fish flakes easily when tested with a fork. Remove from heat; serve fish with slaw. Serves 4 (serving size: 1 fillet and about ½ cup slaw)

SIMPLE SWAP *Make with tilapia or thin-sliced chicken cutlets instead of catfish fillets.*

Calories 256; Fat 12.6g (sat 3.1g, mono 6.5g, poly 2.8g); Protein 26.6g; Carb 6.2g; Fiber 1.5g; Chol 76mg; Iron 0.3mg; Sodium 426mg; Calc 24mg

Crispy Flounder *and* Roasted Tomatoes

HANDS-ON TIME: 18 min. **TOTAL TIME:** 28 min.

Flounder gets a golden crunch from panko, and capers give the tomatoes a briny kick.

- 2 tablespoons capers
- 1 tablespoon olive oil
- 1 pint cherry tomatoes
- ½ teaspoon kosher salt, divided
- ½ teaspoon freshly ground black pepper, divided
- ¼ cup thinly sliced fresh basil
- 1 cup panko (Japanese breadcrumbs)
- 1 tablespoon chopped fresh parsley
- 2 teaspoons chopped fresh thyme
- 4 (6-ounce) skinless flounder fillets
- Cooking spray
- 2 tablespoons olive oil, divided
- Basil leaves (optional)

1 Preheat oven to 400°. Combine first 3 ingredients in a large ovenproof skillet; toss to coat. Sprinkle tomato mixture with ¼ teaspoon salt and ¼ teaspoon pepper. Bake at 400° for 20 minutes. Remove from oven; top with sliced basil.

2 While tomatoes cook, combine panko, parsley, and thyme in a shallow dish. Coat fish with cooking spray; sprinkle with ¼ teaspoon salt and ¼ teaspoon pepper. Dredge fish in panko mixture.

3 Heat a large nonstick skillet over medium-high heat. Add 1 tablespoon oil to pan; swirl to coat. Add 2 fillets to pan; cook 3 minutes on each side or until fish flakes easily when tested with a fork. Repeat procedure with remaining oil and fillets. Serve with tomatoes. Garnish with basil leaves, if desired. Serves 4 (serving size: 1 flounder fillet and ⅓ cup tomatoes)

Calories 317; Fat 13g (sat 1.9g, mono 7.8g, poly 1.7g); Protein 35g; Carb 13.5g; Fiber 1.7g; Chol 82mg; Iron 1.2mg; Sodium 552mg; Calc 48mg

SIMPLE SWAP *Substitute any firm white fish for the flounder. Chopped olives, such as kalamata, will work in place of capers.*

Baked Flounder *with* Fresh Lemon Pepper

HANDS-ON TIME: 8 min. **TOTAL TIME:** 16 min.

PREP TIP *For dinner in a flash, serve with asparagus cooked right along with the fish fillets. Snap the woody bottoms off 1 pound of thin asparagus spears. Toss with 1 tablespoon olive oil and spread in a single layer on a baking sheet. Roast until tender.*

- 2 tablespoons grated lemon rind (about 3 lemons)
- 1 tablespoon extra-virgin olive oil
- 1¼ teaspoons black peppercorns, crushed
- ½ teaspoon salt
- 2 garlic cloves, minced
- 4 (6-ounce) flounder fillets
- Cooking spray
- Lemon wedges (optional)

1 **Preheat oven to 425°.** Combine first 5 ingredients in a small bowl.

2 **Place fish on a jelly-roll pan** coated with cooking spray. Rub garlic mixture evenly over fish.

3 **Bake at 425°** for 8 minutes or until fish flakes easily when tested with a fork. Serve fish with lemon wedges, if desired. Serves 4 (serving size: 1 fillet)

SIMPLE SWAP *Make with skinless halibut fillets instead of flounder.*

Calories 189; Fat 5.4g (sat 0.9g, mono 2.9g, poly 0.9g); Protein 32.2g; Carb 1.2g; Fiber 0.4g; Chol 82mg; Iron 0.8mg; Sodium 432mg; Calc 39mg

SIMPLE SWAP *The flavors of this dish also work well with chicken.*

Halibut à la Provençal *over* Mixed Greens

HANDS-ON TIME: 12 min. **TOTAL TIME:** 18 min.

PREP TIP *Any type of packaged greens should work nicely in this recipe. Vary the mix of lettuces—baby arugula, spring mix, baby spinach—each time you make this. If you like, pair it with garlic bread.*

- 1 teaspoon dried herbes de Provence
- 2 tablespoons fresh lemon juice, divided
- ½ teaspoon salt, divided
- 4 (6-ounce) skinless halibut fillets
- 3 tablespoons olive oil, divided
- ½ teaspoon chopped fresh parsley
- ½ teaspoon chopped fresh thyme

- ¼ cup minced shallots
- 1 teaspoon honey
- ½ teaspoon Dijon mustard
- ¼ teaspoon freshly ground black pepper
- 2 tablespoons finely chopped pitted kalamata olives
- 1 (6-ounce) package mixed salad greens

1 **Combine herbes de Provence,** 2 teaspoons juice, and ¼ teaspoon salt. Rub over tops of fillets.

2 **Heat a large skillet** over medium-high heat. Add 2 teaspoons oil to pan; swirl to coat. Add fish to pan; cook 3 minutes on each side or until fish flakes easily when tested with a fork. Remove fish from pan; sprinkle with parsley and thyme.

3 **Return pan to medium-high heat.** Add 7 teaspoons oil to pan; swirl to coat. Add shallots; sauté 2 minutes or until tender. Remove from heat; stir in 4 teaspoons lemon juice, ¼ teaspoon salt, honey, mustard, and pepper. Stir in olives. Combine greens and dressing in a bowl, tossing well. Serves 4 (serving size: 1 fillet and about 1½ cups mixed greens)

Calories 308; Fat 15.6g (sat 2.2g, mono 9.8g, poly 2.5g); Protein 35.2g; Carb 6.2g; Fiber 1.4g; Chol 52mg; Iron 2.4mg; Sodium 502mg; Calc 115mg

Hazelnut-Crusted Halibut *with* Roasted Asparagus

HANDS-ON TIME: 28 min. **TOTAL TIME:** 28 min.

PREP TIP *Fish is a great choice for quick dinners—most fillets cook to perfection in less than 10 minutes. Serve with roasted red potatoes and asparagus. Thinly slice the potatoes so they'll be done at the same time as the asparagus.*

- 1 tablespoon butter
- 2 teaspoons extra-virgin olive oil, divided
- 4 (6-ounce) skinless halibut fillets
- 1 large egg white, lightly beaten
- ½ teaspoon salt, divided
- ½ teaspoon freshly ground black pepper, divided
- ½ cup finely chopped hazelnuts
- 2 garlic cloves, thinly sliced
- 1 pound asparagus, trimmed
- 1 teaspoon chopped fresh thyme
- 4 lemon wedges

1 **Preheat oven to 400°.** Heat butter and 1 teaspoon oil in a large nonstick skillet over medium-high heat. Brush tops of fish with egg white; sprinkle fish evenly with ¼ teaspoon salt and ¼ teaspoon pepper. Coat tops of fish with nuts, pressing gently to adhere.

2 **Place half of fish,** nuts sides down, in pan; cook 3 minutes or until browned. Turn fish over; cook 4 minutes or until fish flakes easily when tested with a fork. Repeat procedure with remaining fish.

3 **While fish cooks, combine 1 teaspoon oil,** garlic, and asparagus; toss to combine. Sprinkle with ¼ teaspoon salt, ¼ teaspoon pepper, and thyme; spread in a single layer on jelly-roll pan. Bake at 400° for 8 minutes or until crisp-tender. Serve fish with asparagus and lemon wedges. Serves 4 (serving size: 1 fillet, about 5 asparagus spears, and 1 lemon wedge)

Calories 356; Fat 18.1g (sat 3.4g, mono 10.2g, poly 2.8g); Protein 41.2g; Carb 8.2g; Fiber 4g; Chol 62mg; Iron 4.7mg; Sodium 424mg; Calc 131mg

SIMPLE SWAP

Use pecans, walnuts, or pine nuts in place of hazelnuts.

Halibut *with* Caper Salsa Verde *and* Roasted Fennel

HANDS-ON TIME: 13 min. **TOTAL TIME:** 29 min.

PREP TIP *The sweet, mellow flavor of roasted fennel pairs well with halibut. Use a sharp knife to chop the herbs; a dull one will crush them rather than cut them cleanly.*

1 large fennel bulb, cut into ¼-inch-thick slices

2 tablespoons plus 1 teaspoon olive oil, divided

¼ teaspoon kosher salt, divided

³⁄₈ teaspoon freshly ground black pepper, divided

2 tablespoons grated fresh Asiago cheese

2 tablespoons chopped fresh flat-leaf parsley

2 tablespoons chopped fresh basil

1½ teaspoons capers, drained and minced

1 teaspoon minced shallots

¼ teaspoon Dijon mustard

¼ teaspoon grated lemon rind

⅛ teaspoon anchovy paste

2 (6-ounce) skinless halibut fillets

1 **Preheat oven to 400°.** Place fennel in a single layer on a jelly-roll pan; drizzle with 1 tablespoon oil. Sprinkle with ⅛ teaspoon salt and ⅛ teaspoon pepper. Bake at 400° for 12 minutes. Toss fennel with cheese. Bake 12 minutes or until lightly browned and tender.

2 **While fennel roasts, combine 1 tablespoon oil,** ⅛ teaspoon pepper, parsley, and next 6 ingredients (through anchovy paste) in a small bowl, tossing well; set aside.

3 **Heat a large nonstick skillet** over medium-high heat. Add 1 teaspoon oil to pan; swirl to coat. Sprinkle fish evenly with ⅛ teaspoon salt and ⅛ teaspoon pepper. Add fish to pan; cook 4 minutes on each side or until fish flakes easily when tested with a fork. Serves 2 (serving size: 1 fillet, about 2 tablespoons salsa verde, and about ½ cup fennel)

Calories 375; Fat 21g (sat 4.1g, mono 12.5g, poly 2.3g); Protein 40.8g; Carb 4.6g; Fiber 1.9g; Chol 109mg; Iron 1.2mg; Sodium 571mg; Calc 100mg

SIMPLE SWAP

If you can't find baby bok choy, substitute regular.

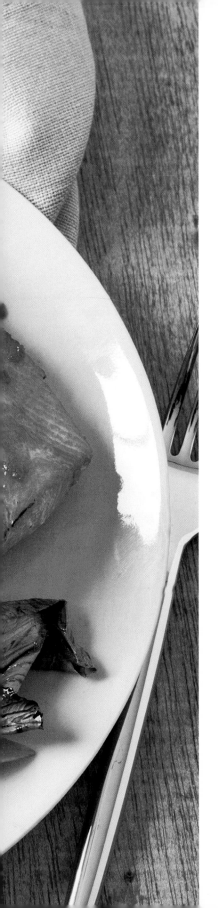

Salmon *and* Bok Choy

HANDS-ON TIME: 11 min. **TOTAL TIME:** 20 min.

PREP TIP

The simple, five-ingredient sauce adds a flavorful finish to the salmon and bok choy. Serve with rice. Put the water on to boil before you preheat the broiler, or prep the rice in the microwave while the main dish cooks.

- 3 tablespoons lower-sodium soy sauce
- 2 tablespoons honey
- 2 teaspoons grated peeled fresh ginger
- 2 teaspoons dark sesame oil
- ½ teaspoon garlic powder
- 1 pound baby bok choy
- 4 (6-ounce) salmon fillets
- ¼ cup diagonally cut green onions

1 **Preheat broiler.** Combine first 5 ingredients in a small bowl, stirring with a whisk.

2 **Coarsely chop bok choy leaves;** arrange in a single layer on one end of a jelly-roll pan. Coarsely chop bok choy stems and arrange in a single layer on opposite end of jelly-roll pan. Place fillets, skin sides down, in a single layer on top of leafy greens. Pour half of soy sauce mixture evenly over fish; pour remaining half evenly over bok choy stems.

3 **Broil 5 minutes;** stir stems. Broil an additional 4 minutes or until fish flakes easily when tested with a fork or until desired degree of doneness. Sprinkle with green onions. Serves 4 (serving size: 1 fillet, ⅓ cup bok choy, and 1 tablespoon green onions)

Calories 320; Fat 13.4g (sat 2g, mono 4.6g, poly 5.4g); Protein 36.3g; Carb 12.8g; Fiber 1.5g; Chol 94mg; Iron 2.5mg; Sodium 444mg; Calc 147mg

Crispy Salmon *and* Arugula Salad *with* Carrot-Ginger Vinaigrette

HANDS-ON TIME: 30 min. **TOTAL TIME:** 30 min.

 SIMPLE SWAP *This dressing is so fresh, so addictive, you might want to spoon it over everything! Try it over chicken, pork, or any type of fish.*

¼ cup grated carrot

3 tablespoons fresh orange juice

2 tablespoons finely chopped onion or shallots, divided

2 tablespoons extra-virgin olive oil, divided

4 teaspoons rice vinegar, divided

1 teaspoon honey

1 teaspoon minced peeled fresh ginger

¾ teaspoon salt, divided

4 ounces baby arugula (about 6 cups loosely packed)

1 cup quartered cherry tomatoes

1 large red bell pepper, thinly sliced

½ teaspoon dark sesame oil

4 (6-ounce) fresh or frozen sustainable salmon fillets (such as wild Alaskan)

¼ teaspoon freshly ground black pepper

1 **Place carrot,** orange juice, 1 tablespoon onion, 1 tablespoon olive oil, 2 teaspoons vinegar, honey, ginger, and ¼ teaspoon salt in a mini food processor; process 1 minute or until well combined.

2 **Place arugula,** tomatoes, and bell pepper in a large bowl. Add 1 tablespoon onion, 1½ teaspoons olive oil, 2 teaspoons vinegar, and sesame oil; toss well. Sprinkle with ¼ teaspoon salt; toss well.

3 **Heat a large nonstick skillet** over medium-high heat. Sprinkle fish with ¼ teaspoon salt and black pepper. Add 1½ teaspoons olive oil to pan; swirl to coat. Add fish to pan, skin sides down; cook 6 minutes or until skin is browned and crisp. Turn fish over; cook 2 minutes or until fish flakes easily when tested with a fork or until desired degree of doneness. Serves 4 (1 fillet, 1½ cups salad, and 2 tablespoons vinaigrette)

Calories 303; Fat 17.1g (sat 2.4g, mono 8.3g, poly 4.8g); Protein 29.7g; Carb 8.9g; Fiber 2.1g; Chol 82mg; Iron 1.5mg; Sodium 536mg; Calc 68mg

Salmon *with* Fiery Asian Slaw

HANDS-ON TIME: 11 min. **TOTAL TIME:** 11 min.

PREP TIP *Be sure to purchase skin-on salmon fillets for the best flavor and texture. If you like, serve with roasted broccoli, which can cook while you prepare the fish and slaw.*

4 (6-ounce) salmon fillets
¾ teaspoon salt, divided
¼ teaspoon freshly ground black pepper
Cooking spray
¼ cup fresh orange juice
1 tablespoon rice vinegar
1 tablespoon balsamic vinegar
1 tablespoon olive oil

2 teaspoons Sriracha (hot chile sauce)
1 teaspoon bottled ground fresh ginger
½ teaspoon honey
½ cup chopped fresh cilantro
1 (16-ounce) package cabbage-and-carrot coleslaw
1 tablespoon toasted sesame seeds

1 Heat a large skillet over medium-high heat. Sprinkle fish evenly with ¼ teaspoon salt and pepper. Coat pan with cooking spray. Add fish to pan, skin sides down; cook 4 minutes.

2 Turn fish over; cook 3 minutes. Add orange juice to pan; cook 30 seconds or until liquid almost evaporates and fish flakes easily when tested with a fork or until desired degree of doneness.

3 While fish cooks, combine rice vinegar and next 5 ingredients (through honey) in a large bowl, stirring with a whisk. Add ½ teaspoon salt, cilantro, and coleslaw; toss well to coat. Sprinkle with sesame seeds. Serve fish with slaw. Serves 4 (serving size: 1 fillet and about 1 cup slaw)

SIMPLE SWAP *Make with skin-on trout fillets instead of salmon.*

Calories 302; Fat 14.8g (sat 2.8g, mono 6.8g, poly 2.8g); Protein 29.2g; Carb 12g; Fiber 3.2g; Chol 65mg; Iron 5.5mg; Sodium 577mg; Calc 66mg

Snapper *with* Zucchini, Tomato, *and* Parsley Orzo

HANDS-ON TIME: 20 min. **TOTAL TIME:** 20 min.

½ cup uncooked orzo (rice-shaped pasta)

2 tablespoons toasted pine nuts

2 teaspoons chopped fresh parsley

5 teaspoons extra-virgin olive oil, divided

½ teaspoon kosher salt, divided

½ teaspoon freshly ground black pepper, divided

2 (6-ounce) snapper fillets

2 tablespoons dry vermouth or white wine

1 cup diced zucchini

1½ tablespoons minced shallots

1 teaspoon chopped fresh oregano

1 teaspoon grated lemon rind

1 cup halved cherry tomatoes

1 tablespoon chopped fresh basil

2 teaspoons fresh lemon juice

1 **Cook orzo** according to package directions, omitting salt and fat. Drain. Stir in pine nuts, parsley, 1 teaspoon extra-virgin olive oil, and ⅛ teaspoon salt. Keep warm.

2 **While orzo cooks, heat a large nonstick skillet** over medium-high heat. Add 1 teaspoon oil to pan; swirl to coat. Sprinkle fish with ¼ teaspoon salt and ¼ teaspoon pepper. Add fish to pan; cook 3 minutes on each side or until fish flakes easily when tested with a fork. Remove fish from pan; keep warm. Add vermouth; cook until liquid almost evaporates. Add zucchini, shallots, oregano, rind, 1 teaspoon oil, and ⅛ teaspoon salt; sauté 3 minutes or until zucchini is tender.

3 **Combine zucchini mixture,** tomatoes, ¼ teaspoon pepper, 2 teaspoons oil, basil, and juice; toss gently. Serve with fish and orzo. Serves 2 (serving size: 1 fillet, 1 cup zucchini mixture, and about ½ cup orzo)

Calories 540; Fat 20.7g (sat 2.5g, mono 10.7g, poly 4.9g); Protein 43.3g; Carb 40.8g; Fiber 3.8g; Chol 63mg; Iron 1.6mg; Sodium 602mg; Calc 86mg

Baked Snapper *with* Chipotle Butter

HANDS-ON TIME: 5 min. **TOTAL TIME:** 20 min.

PREP TIP *Chipotle peppers add a smoky, spicy note to the butter topping. For a cooling side salad, toss diced cucumbers and tomatoes with Greek yogurt.*

½ teaspoon ground cumin
½ teaspoon paprika
¼ teaspoon salt
⅛ teaspoon freshly ground black pepper
4 (6-ounce) red snapper or other firm white fish fillets

Cooking spray
1 tablespoon butter, softened
1 canned chipotle chile in adobo sauce, finely minced
4 lemon wedges

1 **Preheat oven to 400°.** Combine first 4 ingredients in a small bowl; sprinkle evenly over fish.

2 **Place fish on a baking sheet** coated with cooking spray. Bake at 400° for 15 minutes or until fish flakes easily when tested with a fork.

3 **While fish cooks, combine butter** and chile. Spread butter mixture evenly over fish. Serve with lemon wedges. Serves 4 (serving size: 1 fillet and 1 lemon wedge)

SIMPLE SWAP *Tilapia or any other firm white fish would work beautifully with the chipotle butter.*

Calories 203; Fat 5.4g (sat 2.3g, mono 1.3g, poly 0.9g); Protein 35.2g; Carb 1.6g; Fiber 0.4g; Chol 71mg; Iron 0.5mg; Sodium 317mg; Calc 63mg

SIMPLE SWAP

Substitute any firm white fish for the tilapia.

Cumin-Spiced Fish Tacos *with* Avocado-Mango Salsa

HANDS-ON TIME: 23 min. **TOTAL TIME:** 23 min.

PREP TIP *The superb flavor you get from toasting and grinding cumin seeds is well worth the little bit of effort. Clean the grinder to remove flavors that could permeate the next item ground. Sprinkle the tacos with cilantro leaves, if you like.*

- 1 tablespoon cumin seeds
- ¾ teaspoon salt, divided
- ½ teaspoon paprika
- ¼ teaspoon freshly ground black pepper
- 2 garlic cloves, minced
- 1 pound tilapia fillets
- 1 tablespoon canola oil
- 1 cup sliced peeled avocado
- ⅔ cup finely chopped peeled ripe mango
- ¼ cup chopped green onions
- ¼ cup finely chopped red onion
- 2 tablespoons finely chopped fresh cilantro
- 1 tablespoon fresh lime juice
- ¼ teaspoon ground red pepper
- 1 jalapeño pepper, thinly sliced (optional)
- 8 (6-inch) corn tortillas

1 **Heat a large skillet** over medium heat. Add cumin seeds; cook 2 minutes or until toasted, shaking pan frequently. Place cumin, ½ teaspoon salt, paprika, and black pepper in a spice grinder; process until finely ground. Combine cumin mixture and garlic; rub over fish.

2 **Return pan to medium-high heat.** Add oil to pan; swirl to coat. Add fish; cook 2 minutes on each side or until fish flakes easily when tested with a fork. Remove from heat; keep warm. Combine ¼ teaspoon salt, avocado, and next 6 ingredients (through red pepper). Stir in jalapeño, if desired.

3 **Heat tortillas** according to package instructions. Break fish into pieces; divide evenly among tortillas. Top each tortilla with 2 tablespoons salsa. Fold tortillas in half; serve immediately. Serves 4 (serving size: 2 tacos)

Calories 315; Fat 12.4g (sat 1.9g, mono 6.8g, poly 2.8g); Protein 26.2g; Carb 29.1g; Fiber 5.8g; Chol 57mg; Iron 2.1mg; Sodium 521mg; Calc 65mg

Sweet *and* Spicy Citrus Tilapia

HANDS-ON TIME: 9 min. **TOTAL TIME:** 30 min.

PREP TIP *You can save a few minutes by using a quality orange juice instead of squeezing your own. Serve with steamed green beans tossed with chopped fresh cilantro and a generous squeeze of fresh lime juice. Steam the beans and chop the cilantro while the fish marinates.*

4 (6-ounce) tilapia fillets
Cooking spray
½ cup fresh orange juice (about 1 orange)
3 tablespoons fresh lime juice
1 tablespoon brown sugar
1 tablespoon extra-virgin olive oil
2 teaspoons lower-sodium soy sauce

½ teaspoon salt
½ teaspoon ground cumin
¼ teaspoon freshly ground black pepper
¼ teaspoon ground red pepper
2 garlic cloves, crushed
½ teaspoon paprika

1 **Arrange fish** in a single layer in a shallow roasting pan coated with cooking spray. Combine orange juice and next 9 ingredients (through garlic); pour over fish. Let stand 15 minutes.

2 **While fish marinates, preheat broiler.** Sprinkle fish with paprika.

3 **Broil fish 6 minutes** or until fish flakes easily when tested with a fork. Place 1 fillet on each of 4 plates, and drizzle 2 teaspoons sauce evenly over fish. Serves 4

Calories 216; Fat 11.5g (sat 3.1g, mono 5.4g, poly 1.8g); Protein 20.8g; Carb 7.7g; Fiber 2.2g; Chol 35mg; Iron 2.9mg; Sodium 480mg; Calc 54mg

Sautéed Tilapia *with* Salad Greens *and* Honey-Scallion Dressing

HANDS-ON TIME: 15 min. **TOTAL TIME:** 15 min.

 PREP TIP *If you like, serve with fast-cooking noodles on the side. Put water on to boil before making the dressing, and then cook the noodles according to package directions, omitting salt and fat, as you cook the fish.*

2½ tablespoons fresh lemon juice

2 tablespoons chopped green onions

1 tablespoon honey

1 tablespoon lower-sodium soy sauce

1 teaspoon bottled ground fresh ginger

¼ teaspoon dark sesame oil

1 tablespoon canola oil

4 (6-ounce) tilapia fillets

½ teaspoon salt

⅛ teaspoon freshly ground black pepper

4 cups gourmet salad greens

1 Combine first 6 ingredients in a small bowl, stirring well with a whisk.

2 Heat a large nonstick skillet over medium-high heat. Add canola oil to pan; swirl to coat. Sprinkle fish evenly with salt and pepper.

3 Add fish to pan; cook 3 minutes on each side or until fish flakes easily when tested with a fork. Serve fish with greens and dressing. Serves 4 (serving size: 1 fillet, 1 cup greens, and 2 tablespoons dressing)

Calories 230; Fat 7.7g (sat 1.8g, mono 3.9g, poly 1.4g); Protein 34.2g; Carb 7.5g; Fiber 1.4g; Chol 113mg; Iron 1.4mg; Sodium 485mg; Calc 35mg

SIMPLE SWAP

Substitute any firm white fish for the trout.

Pecan-Crusted Trout

HANDS-ON TIME: 18 min. **TOTAL TIME:** 18 min.

PREP TIP *Breading the flesh side of the fish allows the skin to crisp up on the other side. Pair this with steamed sugar snap peas (try Lemony Snap Peas on page 207) and Creamed Spinach and Mushrooms on page 216. Prep the sides before starting the fish.*

- 2 tablespoons all-purpose flour
- ¼ cup nonfat buttermilk
- ⅓ cup pecan halves, ground
- ⅓ cup panko (Japanese breadcrumbs)
- 4 (6-ounce) trout fillets
- ½ teaspoon salt
- ¼ teaspoon freshly ground black pepper
- 1 tablespoon butter, divided
- 1 tablespoon olive oil, divided
- 1 tablespoon chopped fresh parsley
- 4 lemon wedges

1 **Place flour in a shallow dish.** Place buttermilk in a shallow dish. Combine pecans and panko in a shallow dish. Sprinkle fish with salt and pepper. Dredge flesh side of 2 fillets in flour; dip in buttermilk. Dredge in panko mixture.

2 **Melt 1½ teaspoons butter** in a large nonstick skillet over medium-high heat. Add 1½ teaspoons oil to pan; swirl to coat. Add dredged fillets, crust sides down; cook 3 minutes on each side or until fish flakes easily when tested with a fork. Remove from pan; keep warm.

3 **Repeat procedure** with remaining flour, buttermilk, panko mixture, fish, butter, and oil. Top evenly with parsley. Serve with lemon wedges. Serves 4 (serving size: 1 fillet and 1 lemon wedge)

Calories 355; Fat 20.1g (sat 6.3g, mono 7.5g, poly 4.6g); Protein 32.7g; Carb 10.8g; Fiber 1.3g; Chol 106mg; Iron 1mg; Sodium 439mg; Calc 144mg

Sesame Tuna *with* Edamame *and* Soba

HANDS-ON TIME: 27 min. **TOTAL TIME:** 27 min.

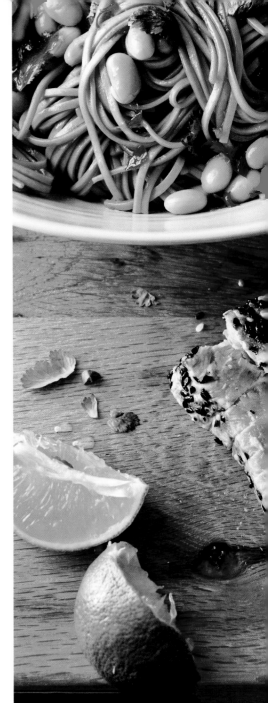

 PREP TIP *Use all white sesame seeds if black seeds are unavailable. Serve with Napa Cabbage Slaw on page 195 for a fresh side with some crunch.*

- **4 ounces soba (Japanese buckwheat noodles)**
- **1 cup frozen shelled edamame (green soybeans)**
- **2 tablespoons lower-sodium soy sauce**
- **1½ tablespoons fresh lime juice**
- **1½ tablespoons sweet chili sauce**
- **1 tablespoon dark sesame oil**
- **¼ cup chopped fresh cilantro**
- **1 tablespoon white sesame seeds**
- **1 tablespoon black sesame seeds**
- **4 (6-ounce) U.S. yellowfin or albacore tuna steaks**
- **Cooking spray**
- **½ teaspoon kosher salt**
- **2 teaspoons canola oil**

1 **Cook soba** according to package directions, omitting salt and fat; add edamame for last 3 minutes. Rinse with warm water; drain well.

2 **Combine soy sauce,** lime juice, chili sauce, and sesame oil in a medium bowl. Add soba mixture and cilantro; keep warm.

3 **Combine white and black sesame seeds** in a shallow dish. Coat fish with cooking spray; sprinkle with salt. Coat both sides of fish with sesame seeds, pressing to adhere. Heat a large nonstick skillet over medium-high heat. Add canola oil to pan; swirl to coat. Add fish; cook 3 minutes on each side or until fish flakes easily when tested with a fork or until desired degree of doneness. Slice fish thinly against grain. Serve with noodles. Serves 4 (serving size: 1 tuna steak and ¾ cup noodles)

 SIMPLE SWAP *You could substitute salmon fillets for the tuna steaks, if you like.*

Calories 413; Fat 11.8g (sat 1.4g, mono 4.1g, poly 3.7g); Protein 50.2g; Carb 26.7g; Fiber 2.6g; Chol 77mg; Iron 4.1mg; Sodium 606mg; Calc 103mg

Greek Tuna Steaks

HANDS-ON TIME: 5 min. **TOTAL TIME:** 30 min.

 PREP TIP *Serve with couscous mixed with crumbled feta cheese, sliced black olives, and chopped tomato. Start the couscous while the tuna marinates. A simple salad of mixed greens tossed with a red wine vinaigrette rounds out the meal. Dress the salad while the tuna cooks.*

1½ teaspoons chopped fresh or ½ teaspoon dried oregano

1 teaspoon olive oil

¾ teaspoon chopped fresh or ¼ teaspoon dried thyme

½ teaspoon salt

¼ teaspoon freshly ground black pepper

4 (6-ounce) U.S. yellowfin or albacore tuna steaks (about ¾ inch thick)

Cooking spray

4 lemon wedges

1 **Combine first 5 ingredients** in a small bowl, and rub evenly over fish. Cover fish, and let stand 15 minutes.

2 **Heat a large grill pan** over medium-high heat. Coat pan with cooking spray.

3 **Add fish to pan,** and cook 5 minutes on each side or until fish flakes easily when tested with a fork or until desired degree of doneness. Serve fish with lemon wedges. Serves 4 (serving size: 1 tuna steak and 1 lemon wedge)

 SIMPLE SWAP *The Mediterranean flavors in this dish are versatile. Striped bass or red snapper fillets would also work nicely.*

Calories 250; Fat 9.7g (sat 2.3g, mono 3.6g, poly 2.7g); Protein 38.2g; Carb 0.2g; Fiber 0.1g; Chol 63mg; Iron 1.8mg; Sodium 357mg; Calc 4mg

SIMPLE SWAP

Make with canned salmon instead of tuna.

Spanish-Style Tuna *and* Potato Salad

HANDS-ON TIME: 11 min. **TOTAL TIME:** 20 min.

 PREP TIP *Look for packaged trimmed haricots verts in the produce section. Save even more time by using packaged pre-cut romaine.*

1 pound small red potatoes, quartered
1 pound haricots verts (French green beans), trimmed and cut into 2-inch pieces
2 cups cherry tomatoes, halved
¼ cup thinly sliced shallots
¾ teaspoon salt
½ teaspoon Spanish smoked paprika
¼ teaspoon ground red pepper
1 (5-ounce) can albacore tuna in water, drained and broken into chunks
¼ cup extra-virgin olive oil
3 tablespoons sherry vinegar
5 cups torn romaine lettuce

1 **Place potatoes** in a large saucepan; cover with water to 2 inches above potatoes. Bring to a boil; cook potatoes 6 minutes or until almost tender. Add beans; cook 4 minutes or until beans are crisp-tender and potatoes are tender. Drain; rinse with cold water. Drain.

2 **Place potato mixture** in a large bowl. Add tomatoes and next 5 ingredients (through tuna); toss. Drizzle potato mixture with oil and vinegar; toss to coat.

3 **Arrange 1 cup lettuce** on each of 5 plates; divide potato mixture evenly among plates. Serves 5

Calories 239; Fat 11.7g (sat 1.6g, mono 7.9g, poly 1.3g); Protein 10.3g; Carb 25.6g; Fiber 6.7g; Chol 10mg; Iron 2mg; Sodium 470mg; Calc 81mg

Roasted Shrimp *and* Broccoli

HANDS-ON TIME: 8 min. **TOTAL TIME:** 17 min.

 Prep your ingredients while the water comes to a boil and the oven preheats. To make this dish even quicker, buy packaged broccoli florets in the produce section. Pair with corn on the cob, which can cook in boiling water while the shrimp and broccoli roast. Purchase fresh, trimmed corn on the cob that has been cleaned of silks.

- 5 **cups broccoli florets**
- 1 **tablespoon grated lemon rind, divided**
- 1 **tablespoon fresh lemon juice**
- ½ **teaspoon salt, divided**
- ½ **teaspoon freshly ground black pepper, divided**
- 1½ **pounds peeled and deveined large shrimp**
- **Cooking spray**
- 2 **tablespoons extra-virgin olive oil**
- ¼ **teaspoon crushed red pepper**

1 **Preheat oven to 425°.** Cook broccoli in boiling water 1 minute. Drain, and plunge into ice water; drain.

2 **Combine 1½ teaspoons rind,** juice, ¼ teaspoon salt, and ¼ teaspoon black pepper in a medium bowl. Add shrimp; toss to combine. Arrange broccoli and shrimp in a single layer on a jelly-roll pan coated with cooking spray. Bake at 425° for 8 minutes or until shrimp are done.

3 **While shrimp and broccoli cook, combine oil,** 1½ teaspoons rind, ¼ teaspoon salt, ¼ teaspoon black pepper, and red pepper in a large bowl. Add shrimp; toss to combine. Serves 4 (serving size: 1 cup broccoli and about 9 shrimp)

Calories 268; Fat 10g (sat 1.5g, mono 5.4g, poly 2g); Protein 37.3g; Carb 7g; Fiber 2.9g; Chol 259mg; Iron 5mg; Sodium 571mg; Calc 135mg

Shrimp *and* Arugula Salad

HANDS-ON TIME: 20 min. **TOTAL TIME:** 20 min.

PREP TIP *As a time-saver, buy packaged matchstick-cut carrots. White balsamic vinegar won't discolor the shrimp or bright veggies. For a little sharper taste, substitute white wine vinegar.*

- 4 cups loosely packed fresh baby arugula
- 1 cup sliced red bell pepper
- ½ cup matchstick-cut carrot
- 3 tablespoons extra-virgin olive oil, divided
- 2 teaspoons minced fresh rosemary
- ½ teaspoon crushed red pepper
- 2 garlic cloves, thinly sliced
- 16 large peeled and deveined shrimp (about ¾ pound)
- 3 tablespoons white balsamic vinegar

1 **Combine** first 3 ingredients in a large bowl; toss gently to combine.

2 **Heat a large skillet** over medium heat. Add 2 tablespoons oil to pan; swirl to coat. Add rosemary, crushed red pepper, and garlic to pan; cook 2 minutes or until garlic is tender, stirring constantly. Increase heat to medium-high. Add shrimp to pan; sauté 6 minutes or until shrimp are done. Remove shrimp mixture from pan.

3 **Add 1 tablespoon oil** and vinegar to pan; cook 15 seconds. Drizzle warm vinegar mixture over arugula mixture; toss gently to coat. Divide arugula mixture among 4 plates; top with shrimp. Serve immediately. Serves 4 (serving size: 1 cup arugula mixture and 4 shrimp)

SIMPLE SWAP

Scallops or chunks of chicken breast can stand in for the shrimp.

Calories 208; Fat 12g (sat 1.7g, mono 7.6g, poly 1.8g); Protein 18.5g; Carb 6.9g; Fiber 1.5g; Chol 129mg; Iron 2.7mg; Sodium 149mg; Calc 101mg

Pan-Fried Shrimp *with* Creole Mayonnaise

HANDS-ON TIME: 15 min. **TOTAL TIME:** 15 min.

Serve with a simple tossed salad of tomato, cucumber, and fennel. Prepare it before you begin the shrimp.

½ cup all-purpose flour

1¼ teaspoons salt-free Creole seasoning, divided

⅛ teaspoon salt

¼ cup fat-free milk

¾ cup dry breadcrumbs

1½ pounds peeled and deveined large shrimp

3 tablespoons olive oil, divided

2 tablespoons canola mayonnaise

1 teaspoon Worcestershire sauce

¼ teaspoon hot sauce

1 **Combine flour,** 1 teaspoon Creole seasoning, and salt in a shallow dish. Pour milk into a shallow dish. Place breadcrumbs in a shallow dish. Dredge shrimp in flour mixture; dip in milk. Dredge shrimp in breadcrumbs; shake off excess breading.

2 **Heat a large nonstick skillet** over medium-high heat. Add 1½ tablespoons oil to pan; swirl to coat. Add half of shrimp; cook 2 minutes on each side or until done. Repeat procedure with remaining oil and shrimp.

3 **Combine mayonnaise,** ¼ teaspoon Creole seasoning, Worcestershire, and hot sauce in a small bowl; stir with a whisk. Serve mayonnaise with shrimp. Serves 4 (serving size: about 5 ounces shrimp and 2 teaspoons mayonnaise)

Calories 427; Fat 19.5g (sat 2.5g, mono 11.3g, poly 4g); Protein 38.4g; Carb 22g; Fiber 0.9g; Chol 261mg; Iron 4.7mg; Sodium 511mg; Calc 111mg

Shrimp *and* Pea Rice Bowl

HANDS-ON TIME: 20 min. **TOTAL TIME:** 20 min.

PREP TIP *To save time, buy shrimp that have already been peeled and deveined.*

1 (8.8-ounce) pouch precooked brown rice

1 tablespoon olive oil

8 ounces medium shrimp, peeled and deveined

3 garlic cloves, minced

¼ cup water

⅔ cup frozen green peas

1 tablespoon white wine vinegar

¾ teaspoon kosher salt

¼ teaspoon crushed red pepper

¼ teaspoon ground turmeric

2 tablespoons chopped fresh flat-leaf parsley

1 **Heat rice** according to package directions; keep warm.

2 **Heat a large skillet** over medium-high heat. Add oil to pan; swirl to coat. Add shrimp to pan; sauté 2 minutes. Add garlic; sauté 1 minute or until shrimp are done. Remove mixture from pan.

3 **Add ¼ cup water to pan;** bring to a simmer. Add peas; cover and cook 2 minutes or until done. Stir in rice, shrimp, vinegar, salt, pepper, and turmeric; cook 1 minute or until heated. Sprinkle with parsley. Serves 3 (serving size: 1 cup)

Calories 280; Fat 8.4g (sat 1.2g, mono 4.4g, poly 2g); Protein 20.2g; Carb 30.5g; Fiber 2.8g; Chol 115mg; Iron 3mg; Sodium 629mg; Calc 55mg

98

Seared Scallops *with* Wilted Watercress *and* Bacon

HANDS-ON TIME: 20 min. **TOTAL TIME:** 20 min.

PREP TIP *Pat the scallops dry with paper towels to ensure you get a beautiful sear.*

- 2 teaspoons canola oil
- 1½ pounds large sea scallops (about 16)
- ³/₈ teaspoon kosher salt, divided
- ¼ teaspoon sugar
- ⅛ teaspoon freshly ground black pepper

- 2 center-cut bacon slices
- ½ cup sliced shallots
- 2 large garlic cloves, thinly sliced
- 3 tablespoons fat-free, lower-sodium chicken broth
- 2 (4-ounce) packages trimmed watercress

1 **Heat a large cast-iron skillet** over medium-high heat. Add oil to pan; swirl to coat. Pat scallops dry with paper towels. Sprinkle both sides of scallops evenly with ¼ teaspoon salt, sugar, and pepper. Add scallops to pan; cook 3 minutes or until done, turning after 2 minutes. Remove from pan; keep warm.

2 **Cook bacon** in a large nonstick skillet over medium heat until crisp. Remove bacon from pan, reserving 2 teaspoons drippings in pan. Crumble bacon.

3 **Add shallots and garlic** to drippings in pan; sauté 2 minutes. Add broth to pan; bring to a boil. Add ⅛ teaspoon salt and watercress to pan; cook 30 seconds or until greens begin to wilt. Place 4 scallops and about 1 cup watercress on each of 4 plates. Sprinkle each serving evenly with bacon. Serves 4

Calories 261; Fat 7.5g (sat 1.7g, mono 3.3g, poly 1.6g); Protein 33.5g; Carb 15.6g; Fiber 0.3g; Chol 63mg; Iron 1.4mg; Sodium 594mg; Calc 112mg

SIMPLE SWAP

Make with peeled and deveined large shrimp instead of scallops.

Pan-Seared Scallops *with* Tomato-Corn Salad

HANDS-ON TIME: 15 min. **TOTAL TIME:** 15 min.

PREP TIP *Look for dry-packed scallops, which will brown best. If you like, pair this dish with sautéed sugar snap peas, which can be prepared at the same time as the corn, in a separate pan.*

1 tablespoon canola oil
1½ pounds sea scallops
¾ teaspoon kosher salt, divided
¼ teaspoon freshly ground black pepper, divided

Cooking spray
2 cups fresh corn kernels (about 3 ears)
2 cups chopped tomato (about 1 pound)
1 cup chopped fresh basil

1 **Heat a large cast-iron** or heavy skillet over high heat. Add oil to pan; swirl to coat.

2 **Pat scallops dry** with paper towels; sprinkle with ½ teaspoon salt and ⅛ teaspoon pepper. Add scallops to pan; cook 2 minutes or until browned. Turn scallops; cook 2 minutes or until done. Remove scallops from pan; keep warm.

3 **Coat pan with cooking spray.** Add corn to pan; sauté 2 minutes or until lightly browned. Remove from heat. Add tomato, basil, ¼ teaspoon salt, and ⅛ teaspoon pepper; toss gently. Serve with scallops. Serves 4 (serving size: about 3 scallops and about 1 cup salad)

Calories 251; Fat 5.7g (sat 0.5g, mono 2.4g, poly 1.9g); Protein 31.6g; Carb 19.4g; Fiber 3.3g; Chol 56mg; Iron 1.4mg; Sodium 641mg; Calc 70mg

Seared Scallops *with* Creamy Cauliflower Puree

HANDS-ON TIME: 16 min. **TOTAL TIME:** 28 min.

 Precut cauliflower florets save you prep work, and the small pieces cook quickly, too. Serve this with sautéed snap peas and carrots.

2 cups chopped cauliflower florets

1 cup cubed peeled Yukon gold potato

1 cup water

½ cup fat-free, lower-sodium chicken broth

1 tablespoon canola oil

1½ pounds sea scallops

¾ teaspoon kosher salt, divided

½ teaspoon coarsely ground black pepper

1½ tablespoons unsalted butter

⅛ teaspoon crushed red pepper

1 **Bring first 4 ingredients** to a boil in a saucepan; cover, reduce heat, and simmer 6 minutes or until potato is tender. Remove from heat. Let stand, uncovered, 10 minutes.

2 **While cauliflower mixture cools, heat a large skillet** over high heat. Add oil to pan; swirl to coat. Pat scallops dry with paper towels; sprinkle with ¼ teaspoon salt and black pepper. Add scallops to pan; cook 3 minutes on each side or until done. Remove scallops from pan.

3 **Pour cauliflower mixture** into a blender. Add ½ teaspoon salt, butter, and red pepper. Remove center piece of blender lid (to allow steam to escape); secure lid on blender. Place a clean towel over opening in lid (to avoid splatters). Blend until smooth. Serve puree with scallops. Serves 4 (serving size: ½ cup puree and about 4 scallops)

Calories 232; Fat 8.9g (sat 3.1g, mono 3.4g, poly 1.5g); Protein 23.8g; Carb 13g; Fiber 2g; Chol 54mg; Iron 1.1mg; Sodium 632mg; Calc 46mg

SIMPLE SWAP

These flavors would go equally well with halibut in place of the scallops.

Curried Coconut Mussels

HANDS-ON TIME: 25 min. **TOTAL TIME:** 30 min.

PREP TIP *Most mussels are farm-raised, so they're easier to clean. You should still take time to rinse them under cold running water, and be sure to remove any beards. Serve with garlic bread to sop up the delicious steaming broth.*

- 1 tablespoon olive oil
- 2 cups chopped onion
- 1 tablespoon finely chopped peeled fresh ginger
- 2 garlic cloves, minced
- 1 jalapeño pepper, chopped
- 2 teaspoons red curry paste
- 1 cup light coconut milk
- ½ cup dry white wine
- 1 teaspoon dark brown sugar
- ¼ teaspoon kosher salt
- 2 pounds small mussels, scrubbed and debearded (about 60)
- ¾ cup small basil leaves, divided
- 3 tablespoons fresh lime juice
- 4 lime wedges

1 **Heat a large Dutch oven** over medium-high heat. Add oil to pan; swirl to coat. Add onion, ginger, garlic, and jalapeño; sauté 3 minutes, stirring frequently. Stir in curry paste; cook 30 seconds, stirring constantly.

2 **Add coconut milk,** wine, sugar, and salt; bring to a boil. Cook 2 minutes. Stir in mussels; cover and cook 5 minutes or until mussels open. Discard any unopened shells. Stir in ½ cup basil and juice.

3 **Divide mussels** among 4 bowls, and spoon coconut mixture evenly over mussels. Sprinkle each serving with basil; serve with lime wedges. Serves 4 (serving size: about 15 mussels, about ½ cup coconut mixture, 1 tablespoon basil, and 1 lime wedge)

Calories 241; Fat 9.9g (sat 4g, mono 3.2g, poly 1.3g); Protein 20g; Carb 19.1g; Fiber 1.7g; Chol 42mg; Iron 6.8mg; Sodium 594mg; Calc 80mg

4

pasta & pizza »

These hearty main dishes
are classic family
favorites guaranteed to
be on the table fast.

To cut costs, swap in chopped almonds or pecans for the pine nuts. Spinach, cauliflower florets, or greens beans would also work nicely here. If you use spinach, simply stir it in when you add the cooked gnocchi to the browned butter.

Browned Butter Gnocchi *with* Broccoli *and* Nuts

HANDS-ON TIME: 10 min. **TOTAL TIME:** 20 min.

PREP TIP *Look for shelf-stable packaged gnocchi with the dried pasta.*

- 2 **(16-ounce) packages prepared gnocchi**
- 5 **cups chopped broccoli florets**
- 2 **tablespoons unsalted butter**
- 2 **tablespoons extra-virgin olive oil**
- ¼ **teaspoon freshly ground black pepper**
- 3 **tablespoons pine nuts, toasted**
- 1.5 **ounces shaved fresh pecorino Romano cheese (about ⅓ cup)**

1 **Cook gnocchi** in a large Dutch oven according to package directions. Add broccoli during last 1 minute of cooking. Drain.

2 **While gnocchi cooks, heat a large skillet** over medium heat. Add butter and oil to pan; cook 7 minutes or until butter browns.

3 **Add gnocchi mixture** and pepper to pan; toss to coat. Spoon about 1½ cups gnocchi mixture into each of 6 shallow bowls. Sprinkle each serving with 1½ teaspoons pine nuts and about 2 teaspoons cheese. Serves 6

Calories 368; Fat 12.8g (sat 3.8g, mono 5.1g, poly 2.2g); Protein 7.9g; Carb 56.6g; Fiber 5.7g; Chol 13mg; Iron 1.2mg; Sodium 614mg; Calc 104mg

Chinese Noodles *with* Tofu *and* Sesame Dressing

HANDS-ON TIME: 25 min. **TOTAL TIME:** 25 min.

PREP TIP *Look for toasted sesame seeds in the spice section of the supermarket. Grab packaged, trimmed snap peas from your produce department.*

1 (8-ounce) package uncooked dried Chinese-style flat noodles

1 cup sugar snap peas, trimmed

2 teaspoons peanut oil

1 cup cubed water-packed firm tofu (about 6 ounces)

1 cup cherry tomatoes, halved

½ cup drained sliced water chestnuts

½ cup thinly sliced green onions

3 tablespoons seasoned rice vinegar

1 tablespoon lower-sodium soy sauce

2 teaspoons dark sesame oil

2 teaspoons chile paste with garlic

¼ teaspoon kosher salt

1 tablespoon toasted sesame seeds, divided

1 **Cook noodles** according to package directions, omitting salt and fat. Add peas during last 1 minute of cooking. Drain; rinse with cold water.

2 **Heat a large nonstick skillet** over medium-high heat. Add peanut oil to pan; swirl to coat. Add tofu; cook 5 minutes or until browned, stirring frequently.

3 **Combine noodle mixture,** tofu, tomatoes, water chestnuts, and onions in a large bowl. Combine vinegar and next 4 ingredients in a bowl, stirring with a whisk. Add vinegar mixture to noodle mixture, tossing gently. Add 1½ teaspoons sesame seeds; toss to combine. Sprinkle with 1½ teaspoons sesame seeds. Serves 4 (serving size: 2 cups)

Calories 351; Fat 10.7g (sat 1.3g, mono 2.8g, poly 3.8g); Protein 14.8g; Carb 55.5g; Fiber 10.2g; Chol 0mg; Iron 7.3mg; Sodium 489mg; Calc 338mg

SIMPLE SWAP

Make with shrimp instead of tofu. If you don't have Chinese-style noodles, use spaghetti or rice noodles.

Farfalle *with* Tomatoes, Onions, *and* Spinach

HANDS-ON TIME: 22 min. **TOTAL TIME:** 23 min.

PREP TIP *Use a vegetable peeler to shave the Parmigiano-Reggiano. Add shredded rotisserie chicken for an even heartier meal.*

- 1 tablespoon plus ¼ teaspoon salt, divided
- 8 ounces uncooked farfalle (bow tie pasta)
- 2 tablespoons extra-virgin olive oil, divided
- 1 cup vertically sliced yellow onion
- 1 teaspoon dried oregano
- 5 garlic cloves, sliced

- 2 cups grape tomatoes, halved
- 1 tablespoon white wine vinegar
- 3 cups fresh baby spinach
- 3 tablespoons shaved fresh Parmigiano-Reggiano cheese
- ¼ teaspoon freshly ground black pepper
- 3 ounces crumbled feta cheese (about ¾ cup)

1 **Bring a large pot** of water to a boil with 1 tablespoon salt. Add pasta, and cook according to package directions. Drain.

2 **While pasta cooks, heat a large non-stick skillet** over medium-high heat. Add 1 tablespoon oil to pan; swirl to coat. Add onion and oregano; sauté 12 minutes or until lightly browned. Add garlic; sauté 2 minutes. Add tomatoes and vinegar; sauté 3 minutes or until tomatoes begin to soften. Add pasta and spinach; cook 1 minute.

3 **Remove from heat,** and stir in Parmigiano-Reggiano, 1 tablespoon oil, ¼ teaspoon salt, and pepper. Sprinkle with feta. Serves 4 (serving size: about 1½ cups pasta mixture and 3 tablespoons feta)

Calories 374; Fat 13.3g (sat 5g, mono 6.2g, poly 0.9g); Protein 13.7g; Carb 51.1g; Fiber 3.8g; Chol 22mg; Iron 2.6mg; Sodium 632mg; Calc 212mg

Baked Mac *and* Cheese

HANDS-ON TIME: 10 min. **TOTAL TIME:** 33 min.

PREP TIP *Blending the cottage cheese creates a smooth, silky sauce. You can assemble this casserole, untopped, up to a day ahead. Serve with a spinach salad topped with sliced red onion and grape tomatoes.*

12 ounces uncooked penne (tube-shaped pasta)

1 (12-ounce) carton 2% low-fat cottage cheese

2 ounces finely shredded sharp cheddar cheese (about ½ cup)

2 ounces grated fresh Parmesan cheese (about ½ cup), divided

½ teaspoon salt

⅛ teaspoon freshly ground black pepper

Cooking spray

3 tablespoons panko (Japanese bread-crumbs)

1 tablespoon minced fresh flat-leaf parsley

1 **Preheat oven to 375°.** Cook pasta according to package directions, omitting salt and fat. Drain; place in a large bowl.

2 **While pasta cooks, place cottage cheese** in a food processor; process until smooth. Combine cottage cheese, cheddar cheese, 1 ounce Parmesan cheese, salt, and pepper. Add cheese mixture to pasta; stir well. Spoon mixture into an 11 x 7-inch glass or ceramic baking dish coated with cooking spray. Combine 1 ounce Parmesan, panko, and parsley in a small bowl. Sprinkle evenly over pasta mixture. Bake at 375° for 10 minutes.

3 **Preheat broiler** (do not remove dish from the oven). Broil 1 minute or until top browns. Serves 6 (serving size: about 1⅓ cups)

Calories 329; Fat 7.4g (sat 4.4g, mono 0.8g, poly 0.1g); Protein 19.1g; Carb 47g; Fiber 1.9g; Chol 21mg; Iron 2mg; Sodium 455mg; Calc 275mg

Fettuccine *with* Tomato-Cream Sauce

HANDS-ON TIME: 25 min. **TOTAL TIME:** 25 min.

 Adding a bit of salt to the boiling water enhances the flavor of the pasta, but have a light hand. The saltier the pasta water, the saltier the pasta.

- 8 ounces uncooked fettuccine
- 4 quarts boiling water
- ½ teaspoon kosher salt, divided
- 1 tablespoon olive oil
- 3 tablespoons coarsely chopped garlic
- 1 (28-ounce) can whole peeled tomatoes, drained and crushed
- 3 ounces ⅓-less-fat cream cheese
- ¼ cup oil-cured olives, pitted and coarsely chopped
- ¼ teaspoon crushed red pepper
- ¼ cup small basil leaves
- ½ ounce shaved fresh Parmigiano-Reggiano cheese

 Cook pasta in 4 quarts boiling water with ¼ teaspoon salt 8 minutes or until pasta is almost al dente. Drain through a sieve over a bowl; reserve 1⅓ cups pasta cooking water.

Heat a large skillet over medium-low heat. Add oil to pan; swirl to coat. Add garlic; cook 2 minutes or until very fragrant and tender, stirring occasionally. Stir in ¼ teaspoon salt and tomatoes; cook 3 minutes, stirring occasionally. Stir in reserved 1⅓ cups pasta water; bring to a boil.

 Add cream cheese; stir until smooth. Add pasta, olives, and red pepper; cook 3 minutes or until pasta is al dente. Divide pasta mixture among 4 bowls; top each with 1 tablespoon basil. Divide Parmigiano-Reggiano evenly among servings. Serves 4 (serving size 1¼ cups)

 Use whatever type of pasta you have on hand.

Calories 383; Fat 14.2g (sat 4.5g, mono 7.1g, poly 1.2g); Protein 12.9g; Carb 52.7g; Fiber 3.6g; Chol 19mg; Iron 3.6mg; Sodium 533mg; Calc 142mg

Easy Penne *with* Tuna

HANDS-ON TIME: 12 min. **TOTAL TIME:** 40 min.

 PREP TIP *If you're short on time, you can get this on the table quicker by using bottled roasted red peppers instead of roasting your own. Pair this dish with crusty bread to make it a complete dinner.*

1 large red bell pepper
4 quarts water
2¼ teaspoons salt, divided
6 ounces uncooked penne (tube-shaped pasta)
2 cups coarsely chopped arugula
¼ cup thinly sliced shallots

2 tablespoons red wine vinegar
1 tablespoon capers, drained
1 tablespoon extra-virgin olive oil
1 (7.8-ounce) jar premium tuna packed in oil, drained and flaked

1 **Preheat broiler.** Cut bell pepper in half lengthwise; discard seeds and membranes. Place pepper halves, skin sides up, on a foil-lined baking sheet; flatten with hand. Broil 15 minutes or until blackened. Place in a zip-top plastic bag; seal. Let stand 15 minutes. Peel and chop.

2 **While peppers stand, bring 4 quarts** water and 2 teaspoons salt to a boil in a large saucepan. Cook pasta according to package directions, omitting additional salt and fat. Drain and rinse with cold water; drain well.

3 **Combine bell pepper,** pasta, ¼ teaspoon salt, arugula, and remaining ingredients in a large bowl; toss well. Serves 4 (serving size: 2 cups)

Calories 310; Fat 8.8g (sat 1.4g, mono 4.3g, poly 2.3g); Protein 21.4g; Carb 36.3g; Fiber 2.5g; Chol 17mg; Iron 2.2mg; Sodium 556mg; Calc 34mg

Tuna Noodle Casserole

HANDS-ON TIME: 24 min. **TOTAL TIME:** 32 min.

PREP TIP *This is a delicious way to get your kids to eat their vegetables; increase the carrots and peas as much as suits your family's taste. Serve with a salad tossed with your favorite vinaigrette to balance the creaminess of the casserole.*

- 8 ounces uncooked wide egg noodles
- 2 tablespoons olive oil
- ½ cup chopped yellow onion
- ⅓ cup chopped carrot
- 2 tablespoons all-purpose flour
- 2¾ cups fat-free milk
- 4 ounces ⅓-less-fat cream cheese (about ½ cup), softened
- 2 tablespoons Dijon mustard
- ½ teaspoon freshly ground black pepper
- ¼ teaspoon salt
- 1 cup frozen green peas, thawed
- 2 ounces grated fresh Parmigiano-Reggiano cheese (about ½ cup), divided
- 2 (5-ounce) cans albacore tuna in water, drained and flaked
- Cooking spray

1 **Preheat broiler.** Cook noodles according to package directions, omitting salt and fat.

2 **While noodles cook, heat a skillet** over medium heat. Add oil to pan; swirl. Add onion and carrot; cook 6 minutes or until carrot is almost tender. Sprinkle with flour; cook 1 minute, stirring constantly. Gradually stir in milk; cook 5 minutes, stirring constantly until slightly thick. Stir in cream cheese, mustard, pepper, and salt; cook 2 minutes, stirring constantly.

3 **Remove pan from heat.** Stir in noodles, peas, ¼ cup Parmigiano-Reggiano, and tuna. Spoon mixture into a broiler-safe 2-quart baking dish coated with cooking spray; top with ¼ cup Parmigiano-Reggiano. Broil 3 minutes or until golden and bubbly. Let stand 5 minutes. Serves 6 (serving size: 1⅓ cups)

Calories 422; Fat 16.5g (sat 7.1g, mono 6.3g, poly 1.8g); Protein 27.4g; Carb 40.6g; Fiber 3g; Chol 88mg; Iron 2.4mg; Sodium 608mg; Calc 293mg

Shrimp Florentine Pasta

HANDS-ON TIME: 14 min. **TOTAL TIME:** 23 min.

 PREP TIP *Lemon juice adds bright acidity and makes all the difference in such a simple dish. Garnish with a slice of lemon to enhance the citrus effect. To save 10 minutes of prep time, buy already peeled and deveined shrimp.*

8 ounces uncooked fettuccine

2 tablespoons butter

1 pound large shrimp, peeled and deveined

1 tablespoon chopped fresh garlic

1 teaspoon crushed red pepper

1 tablespoon fresh lemon juice

½ teaspoon kosher salt

½ teaspoon freshly ground black pepper

1 (6-ounce) package fresh baby spinach

1 **Cook pasta** according to package directions, omitting salt and fat. Drain well; set aside, and keep warm.

2 **While pasta cooks, melt butter** in a large nonstick skillet over medium heat; swirl to coat. Add shrimp, garlic, and red pepper to pan; cook 4 minutes or until shrimp are done, stirring occasionally.

3 **Add pasta,** juice, salt, black pepper, and spinach to pan; cook 3 minutes or until spinach starts to wilt, stirring to combine. Serves 4 (serving size: 1¾ cups)

 SIMPLE SWAP *Thinly sliced skinless, boneless chicken breast is a delicious substitute for the shrimp. The cook time will vary, so be certain to cook the chicken all the way through.*

Calories 402; Fat 8.6g (sat 4.3g, mono 1.8g, poly 1g); Protein 32.1g; Carb 49.3g; Fiber 4g; Chol 188mg; Iron 6mg; Sodium 520mg; Calc 107mg

Soy-Citrus Scallops *with* Soba Noodles

HANDS-ON TIME: 10 min. **TOTAL TIME:** 20 min.

 PREP TIP *Serve with snow peas or sugar snap peas for some fresh crunch. Toss them right in with the noodles.*

- 6 ounces uncooked soba (Japanese buckwheat noodles)
- 3 tablespoons lower-sodium soy sauce
- 1 tablespoon dark sesame oil, divided
- 1 tablespoon fresh orange juice
- 1 tablespoon rice vinegar
- 1 tablespoon honey
- ½ teaspoon minced peeled fresh ginger
- ¼ teaspoon chili garlic sauce
- 1 pound large sea scallops (12 scallops)
- ¼ cup thinly sliced green onions
- ⅛ teaspoon salt

1 **Cook noodles** according to package directions, omitting salt and fat.

2 **While noodles cook, combine soy sauce,** 1 teaspoon oil, and next 5 ingredients (through chili garlic sauce) in a shallow glass or ceramic baking dish; add scallops to dish in a single layer. Marinate 4 minutes on each side.

3 **Heat a skillet** over medium-high heat. Add 2 teaspoons oil; swirl. Remove scallops from dish, reserving marinade. Add scallops to pan; sauté 1 minute on each side or until almost done. Remove scallops from pan; keep warm. Place marinade in pan; bring to a boil. Return scallops to pan; cook 1 minute. Toss noodles with green onions and salt. Place 1 cup noodle mixture on each of 4 plates. Top each with 3 scallops, and drizzle with 1 tablespoon sauce. Serves 4

 SIMPLE SWAP *You can also prepare this with shrimp, if you like.*

Calories 315; Fat 4.5g (sat 0.6g, mono 1.5g, poly 1.5g); Protein 28g; Carb 42.7g; Fiber 1.9g; Chol 37mg; Iron 1.3mg; Sodium 653mg; Calc 41mg

Greek Pasta *with* Meatballs

HANDS-ON TIME: 16 min. **TOTAL TIME:** 32 min.

PREP TIP *Sharp, tangy feta cheese is a fitting complement to spiced lamb. You can brown the meatballs, freeze on a baking sheet, transfer to a zip-top plastic bag, and store in the freezer for up to a month.*

2 cups hot cooked orzo
⅓ cup plain dry breadcrumbs
½ teaspoon dried oregano
¼ teaspoon salt
¼ teaspoon ground cinnamon
¼ teaspoon freshly ground black pepper
1 pound lean ground lamb

1 garlic clove, minced
2 tablespoons chopped fresh parsley, divided
2 large egg whites
1½ teaspoons olive oil
2 cups lower-sodium marinara sauce
3 ounces crumbled feta cheese (about ¾ cup)

1 **Preheat oven to 375°.** Cook pasta according to package directions; drain. Keep warm.

2 **While pasta cooks, combine breadcrumbs** and next 6 ingredients (through garlic) in a medium bowl; stir in 1½ tablespoons parsley. Add egg whites, stirring mixture until just combined. Shape mixture into 12 (1-inch) meatballs; cover and chill meatballs 5 minutes.

3 **Heat a large ovenproof skillet** over medium-high heat. Add oil to pan; swirl to coat. Add meatballs to pan; cook 8 minutes, turning to brown on all sides. Drain well; wipe pan clean with paper towels. Return meatballs to pan. Spoon marinara sauce over meatballs; sprinkle with cheese. Bake at 375° for 11 minutes or until meatballs are done. Sprinkle with 1½ teaspoons parsley. Serve over orzo. Serves 4 (serving size: ½ cup orzo, 3 meatballs, and ½ cup sauce)

Calories 260; Fat 7.2g (sat 2.3g, mono 3.1g, poly 1.4g); Protein 29.1g; Carb 19.8g; Fiber 0.9g; Chol 53mg; Iron 1.9mg; Sodium 332mg; Calc 10mg

Pasta Pork Bolognese

HANDS-ON TIME: 14 min. **TOTAL TIME:** 14 min.

PREP TIP *Serve this with steamed sugar snap peas or Citrus Green Beans with Pine Nuts (page 205). They can cook at the same time as the sauce.*

1 (9-ounce) package refrigerated fettuccine

2 teaspoons olive oil

12 ounces lean ground pork

½ cup grated carrot

3 garlic cloves, minced

⅓ cup red wine

1⅔ cups lower-sodium marinara sauce

½ cup thinly sliced fresh basil, divided

½ teaspoon kosher salt

¼ teaspoon freshly ground black pepper

1 **Cook pasta** according to package directions, omitting salt and fat. Drain.

2 **While pasta cooks, heat a large skillet** over medium-high heat. Add oil to pan; swirl to coat. Add pork, carrot, and garlic; sauté 4 minutes or until pork is done.

3 **Add wine to pan;** cook 1 minute. Add marinara, ¼ cup basil, salt, and pepper; bring to a simmer. Pour sauce over pasta. Sprinkle with ¼ cup basil. Serves 4 (serving size: 1¼ cups)

Calories 412; Fat 13.1g (sat 4.6g, mono 5.1g, poly 1g); Protein 24.9g; Carb 67.6g; Fiber 2.1g; Chol 102mg; Iron 1.7mg; Sodium 468mg; Calc 35mg

Garlicky Meatball Pasta

HANDS-ON TIME: 20 min. **TOTAL TIME:** 31 min.

PREP TIP *Serve this with Lemony Snap Peas (page 207) or make a simple spinach salad tossed with your favorite dressing while the meatballs cook.*

1 (9-ounce) package refrigerated fettuccine	2 garlic cloves, minced
12 ounces ground sirloin	1 large egg, lightly beaten
½ cup panko (Japanese breadcrumbs)	2 teaspoons olive oil
⅓ cup chopped fresh basil	1¾ cups lower-sodium marinara sauce
⅜ teaspoon kosher salt	1 ounce grated fresh Parmesan cheese (about ¼ cup)
¼ teaspoon freshly ground black pepper	

1 **Cook pasta** according to package directions, omitting salt and fat. Drain through a sieve over a bowl, and reserve ⅓ cup cooking liquid.

2 **While pasta cooks, combine beef** and next 6 ingredients (through egg); shape mixture into 16 meatballs. Heat a large skillet over medium-high heat. Add oil to pan; swirl to coat. Add meatballs; cook 5 minutes, browning on all sides.

3 **Reduce heat to medium-low.** Add marinara and reserved ⅓ cup pasta water. Cover, and cook 11 minutes or until meatballs are done. Divide pasta evenly among 4 plates; top evenly with sauce, meatballs, and cheese. Serves 4

SIMPLE SWAP *Make the meatballs with a combination of ground beef and pork, or all ground turkey.*

SIMPLE SWAP

Sub lean ground beef or turkey for the pork.

Calories 489; Fat 16.6g (sat 6.1g, mono 6.9g, poly 1g); Protein 29.1g; Carb 71.6g; Fiber 2.6g; Chol 147mg; Iron 2.4mg; Sodium 688mg; Calc 110mg

SIMPLE SWAP

You can substitute ground chicken or pork if you have that on hand.

Spanish Spaghetti *with* Olives

HANDS-ON TIME: 24 min. **TOTAL TIME:** 39 min.

PREP TIP *Serve with a salad topped with sliced pear, chopped walnuts, and shaved Parmesan cheese for a sweet finish. Squeeze lemon on the cut pear to keep it from browning. Toss it together while the sauce simmers.*

- 8 ounces uncooked thin spaghetti
- 1 tablespoon olive oil
- 2 cups chopped onion
- 2 teaspoons minced fresh garlic
- 1 teaspoon dried oregano
- ½ teaspoon celery salt
- ¼ teaspoon crushed red pepper
- ¼ teaspoon freshly ground black pepper
- ¼ teaspoon crushed saffron threads (optional)
- 8 ounces extra-lean ground beef
- 1²/₃ cups lower-sodium marinara sauce
- 2 ounces pimiento-stuffed olives, sliced (about ½ cup)
- ¼ cup dry sherry
- 1 tablespoon capers
- ¼ cup chopped fresh parsley, divided

Cook pasta according to package directions, omitting salt and fat; drain.

While pasta cooks, heat a large skillet over medium-high heat. Add oil to pan; swirl to coat. Add onion to pan; sauté 4 minutes or until tender. Add garlic; sauté 1 minute. Stir in oregano, celery salt, red pepper, black pepper, and saffron, if desired. Crumble beef into pan; cook 5 minutes or until beef is browned, stirring to crumble.

3 Stir in marinara sauce, olives, sherry, capers, and 3 tablespoons parsley. Bring to a boil; reduce heat, and simmer 15 minutes. Add spaghetti to sauce mixture. Cook 2 minutes or until thoroughly heated. Sprinkle with 1 tablespoon parsley. Serves 4 (serving size: about 1¾ cups)

Calories 407; Fat 9.3g (sat 2g, mono 4.6g, poly 0.8g); Protein 21g; Carb 57.1g; Fiber 4.6g; Chol 30mg; Iron 4.9mg; Sodium 606mg; Calc 69mg

Chili-Cheese Mac

HANDS-ON TIME: 13 min. **TOTAL TIME:** 20 min.

 PREP TIP *Adjust the spice level to suit your taste; if you like, amp up the chili powder for some added heat.*

SIMPLE SWAP *Use ground turkey instead of beef, and Monterey Jack (with jalapeño peppers, if you like) instead of cheddar.*

1 teaspoon canola oil
¾ pound ground round
2 teaspoons chili powder
1 teaspoon garlic powder
1 teaspoon ground coriander
1 teaspoon ground cumin
2 cups fat-free, lower-sodium beef broth
1 cup water

1 (10-ounce) can mild diced tomatoes and green chiles, undrained
8 ounces uncooked elbow macaroni
½ cup fat-free milk
4 ounces ⅓-less-fat cream cheese (about ½ cup)
4½ ounces finely shredded reduced-fat sharp cheddar cheese (about 1⅛ cups)

 1 **Heat a Dutch oven** over medium-high heat. Add oil to pan; swirl to coat. Add beef and next 4 ingredients (through cumin); cook 3 minutes. Add broth, 1 cup water, and tomatoes; bring to a boil. Stir in macaroni; cover and cook 10 minutes or until macaroni is done.

 2 **While pasta cooks, heat milk** and cream cheese in a saucepan over medium heat. Cook 4 minutes or until cheese melts, stirring frequently. Remove from heat.

3 **Stir in cheddar cheese.** Add cheese sauce to pasta mixture; toss well to coat. Serves 6 (serving size: 1 cup)

Calories 342; Fat 12.3g (sat 6g, mono 3.7g, poly 1.1g); Protein 25.7g; Carb 32.7g; Fiber 1.8g; Chol 60mg; Iron 2.3mg; Sodium 652mg; Calc 363mg

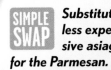

SIMPLE SWAP *Substitute less expensive asiago for the Parmesan.*

Creamy Grilled Chicken Pasta

HANDS-ON TIME: 20 min. **TOTAL TIME:** 40 min.

Refrigerated fresh linguine cooks in under four minutes, so use it when you're in a hurry. Pair this pasta with Broccolini. You can grill it alongside the chicken for an easy side dish.

2 (6-ounce) bone-in chicken breasts halves, skinned
¾ teaspoon salt, divided
¾ teaspoon freshly ground black pepper, divided
Cooking spray
8 ounces uncooked linguine
2 tablespoons canola oil
3 tablespoons all-purpose flour

1 teaspoon chopped fresh garlic
1 cup whole milk
1 cup fat-free, lower-sodium chicken broth
3 ounces grated fresh Parmesan cheese (about ¾ cup)
4 cups fresh spinach leaves

1 **Preheat grill** to medium-high heat. Sprinkle chicken with ¼ teaspoon salt and ¼ teaspoon pepper. Place chicken on grill rack coated with cooking spray, and grill 8 minutes on each side or until done. Let stand 10 minutes. Carve chicken off bones, and thinly slice.

2 **While chicken cooks, cook pasta** according to package directions, omitting salt and fat. Drain well; keep warm.

3 **Heat a large nonstick skillet** over medium-high heat. Add oil to pan; swirl to coat. Add flour and garlic; cook 2 minutes or until garlic is browned, stirring constantly. Add milk and broth, stirring with a whisk; bring to a simmer, and cook 2 minutes or until thick. Add cheese, stirring until cheese melts. Add ½ teaspoon salt, ½ teaspoon pepper, and spinach; stir until spinach wilts. Add pasta and chicken; toss to combine. Serves 4 (serving size: about 1½ cups)

Calories 332; Fat 10.3g (sat 3.2g, mono 4.3g, poly 1.7g); Protein 24.8g; Carb 35g; Fiber 2g; Chol 46mg; Iron 2.6mg; Sodium 579mg; Calc 195mg

SIMPLE SWAP

Angel hair is a great quick-cooking option, but feel free to use whatever pasta you have on hand.

Chicken Puttanesca

HANDS-ON TIME: 20 min. **TOTAL TIME:** 20 min.

 Serve with crusty bread, which you can toast under the broiler while the sauce cooks.

8 ounces uncooked angel hair pasta	¼ cup sliced green olives
1½ tablespoons olive oil, divided	1 tablespoon chopped fresh oregano
4 (4-ounce) skinless, boneless chicken breast cutlets	1½ teaspoons capers, chopped
¼ cup minced fresh onion	½ teaspoon crushed red pepper
3 garlic cloves, minced	¼ teaspoon salt
2 cups chopped tomato	1 canned anchovy fillet, chopped

1 **Cook pasta** according to package directions, omitting salt and fat. Drain.

2 **While pasta cooks, heat a large non-stick skillet** over medium-high heat. Add 1 tablespoon oil to pan; swirl to coat. Add chicken to pan; cook 5 minutes or until done, turning once. Remove chicken from pan; keep warm.

3 **Add 1½ teaspoons oil,** onion, and garlic to pan; sauté 1 minute. Add tomato and remaining ingredients. Bring to a simmer, and cook 9 minutes or until sauce is slightly thick, stirring occasionally. Serve chicken with tomato mixture over pasta. Serves 4 (serving size: 1 chicken cutlet, about ⅓ cup tomato mixture, and about ¾ cup pasta)

Calories 448; Fat 12.8g (sat 1.7g, mono 6.6g, poly 2.4g); Protein 36.4g; Carb 479g; Fiber 3.3g; Chol 94mg; Iron 2.4mg; Sodium 663mg; Calc 38mg

White Pizza *with* Tomato *and* Basil

HANDS-ON TIME: 15 min. **TOTAL TIME:** 20 min.

 PREP TIP *Fresh mozzarella is easier to shred when it is very firm, so freeze it until firm, and then shred. Heating a baking sheet in the oven before you put the pizza on it gives you a crisper crust.*

- 1 (10-ounce) prebaked Italian cheese-flavored thin pizza crust
- 1 teaspoon cornmeal
- Cooking spray
- 3 tablespoons commercial pesto
- 2 ounces shredded fresh mozzarella cheese (about ½ cup)

- ½ cup part-skim ricotta cheese
- ½ cup sliced small tomatoes (such as Campari tomatoes)
- ¼ cup small basil leaves
- ¼ teaspoon freshly ground black pepper
- Crushed red pepper (optional)

 1 **Preheat broiler.** Place a baking sheet in oven; heat 10 minutes.

 2 **While baking sheet heats, place crust** on another baking sheet sprinkled with cornmeal. Lightly coat crust with cooking spray. Spread pesto evenly over crust, leaving a 1-inch border; sprinkle mozzarella evenly over pesto. Top pizza with teaspoonfuls of ricotta. Slide pizza onto preheated baking sheet, using a spatula as a guide. Broil 5 inches from heat 5 minutes or until cheese begins to melt.

3 **Remove pizza from oven;** top evenly with tomatoes, basil, and black pepper. Sprinkle with red pepper, if desired. Cut into 8 slices. Serves 4 (serving size: 2 slices)

Calories 352; Fat 13.8g (sat 4.8g, mono 3.2g, poly 3.2g); Protein 15.8g; Carb 40.2g; Fiber 2g; Chol 24mg; Iron 2.6mg; Sodium 643mg; Calc 297mg

Roasted Vegetable *and* Ricotta Pizza

HANDS-ON TIME: 11 min. **TOTAL TIME:** 48 min.

 PREP TIP *To save prep time, buy presliced cremini mushrooms, and use a prebaked pizza crust instead of fresh pizza dough.*

- 1 pound refrigerated fresh pizza dough
- 2 cups sliced cremini mushrooms
- 1 cup (¼-inch) sliced zucchini
- ¼ teaspoon freshly ground black pepper
- 1 medium yellow bell pepper, sliced
- 1 medium red onion, cut into thick slices
- 5½ teaspoons olive oil, divided
- 1 tablespoon yellow cornmeal
- ⅓ cup tomato sauce
- 4 ounces shredded part-skim mozzarella cheese (about 1 cup)
- ½ teaspoon crushed red pepper
- ⅓ cup part-skim ricotta cheese
- 2 tablespoons small basil leaves

1 **Remove dough** from refrigerator. Let stand, covered, 30 minutes. Position an oven rack in lowest setting; place a baking sheet or pizza stone on rack. Preheat oven to 500°.

2 **While dough stands, combine mushrooms** and next 4 ingredients (through onion) in a large bowl; drizzle with 1½ tablespoons oil. Toss. Arrange vegetables on a jelly-roll pan. Bake at 500° for 15 minutes.

3 **Sprinkle** a lightly floured baking sheet with cornmeal; roll dough out to a 15-inch circle on prepared baking sheet. Brush dough with 1 teaspoon oil. Spread sauce over dough, leaving a ½-inch border. Sprinkle with ½ cup mozzarella; top with vegetables. Sprinkle with ½ cup mozzarella and red pepper. Dollop with ricotta. Slide pizza onto preheated baking sheet. Bake at 500° for 11 minutes or until crust is golden. Sprinkle with basil. Cut into 12 slices. Serves 6 (serving size: 2 slices)

Calories 347; Fat 11.1g (sat 3.7g, mono 4.4g, poly 2g); Protein 14.8g; Carb 48.5g; Fiber 2.7g; Chol 15mg; Iron 3mg; Sodium 655mg; Calc 193mg

Winter Greens, Asiago, *and* Anchovy Pizza

HANDS-ON TIME: 15 min. **TOTAL TIME:** 35 min.

 PREP TIP *Anchovies and raisins, a popular eastern Mediterranean pairing, bring a salty sweetness to this calcium-rich pizza.*

Cooking spray
1 cup sliced red onion (about 1 medium)
3 tablespoons raisins
3 garlic cloves, minced
2 canned anchovy fillets, minced
3 cups loosely packed fresh baby spinach (about 3 ounces)
3 cups chopped turnip greens (about 5 ounces)

¼ teaspoon crushed red pepper
1 (10-ounce) Italian cheese-flavored thin pizza crust
3 ounces shredded part-skim mozzarella cheese (about ¾ cup)
2 ounces grated fresh Asiago cheese (about ½ cup)

1 **Preheat oven to 400°.** Heat a large skillet over medium heat. Coat pan with cooking spray. Add onion, and cook 10 minutes or until tender, stirring occasionally. Add raisins, garlic, and anchovies; cook 2 minutes, stirring frequently. Add spinach and greens; cover and cook 4 minutes or until spinach and greens wilt. Uncover and cook 3 minutes or until liquid evaporates. Stir in pepper. Cool slightly.

2 **Place crust** on a baking sheet. Sprinkle crust evenly with mozzarella; top evenly with spinach mixture. Sprinkle Asiago evenly over spinach mixture.

3 **Bake at 400° for 12 minutes** or until cheese melts and begins to brown. Cut into 8 slices. Serves 4 (serving size: 2 slices)

Calories 391; Fat 13.1g (sat 5.9g, mono 3.3g, poly 3g); Protein 20g; Carb 49.6g; Fiber 3.9g; Chol 26mg; Iron 4.3mg; Sodium 833mg; Calc 528mg

Steak House Pizza

HANDS-ON TIME: 30 min. **TOTAL TIME:** 30 min.

 PREP TIP *If the dough starts retracting and fighting you as you shape it, walk away for a couple of minutes; let it relax, and it will cooperate.*

- 1 pound refrigerated fresh pizza dough
- 8 teaspoons olive oil, divided
- 2 garlic cloves, minced
- 2 (4-ounce) beef tenderloin steaks
- ⅛ teaspoon kosher salt
- 4 cups loosely packed arugula
- ¼ cup thinly sliced red onion
- 3 tablespoons balsamic vinaigrette
- 2 ounces crumbled blue cheese (about ½ cup)
- ¼ teaspoon freshly ground black pepper

1 **Preheat oven to 450°.** Place dough in a microwave-safe bowl; microwave at MEDIUM (50% power) 45 seconds. Let stand 5 minutes. Roll dough into a 14-inch circle. Place on a pizza pan; pierce with a fork. Combine 2 tablespoons oil and garlic; brush over dough. Bake at 450° for 14 minutes.

2 **While dough bakes, heat a large skillet** over medium-high heat. Add 2 teaspoons oil to pan; swirl to coat. Sprinkle steaks with salt. Add steaks to pan; cook 3 minutes on each side. Remove from pan; let stand 5 minutes. Cut across grain into slices.

3 **While steaks stand, combine arugula,** onion, and vinaigrette. Arrange over crust; top with steak, cheese, and pepper. Cut into 12 slices. Serves 6 (serving size: 2 slices)

 SIMPLE SWAP

Substitute spinach for the arugula and feta for the blue cheese.

Calories 360; Fat 14.6g (sat 3.7g, mono 6.8g, poly 1.2g); Protein 17.3g; Carb 37.4g; Fiber 5.7g; Chol 30mg; Iron 1.8mg; Sodium 564mg; Calc 80mg

Bacon, Onion, *and* Mushroom Pizza

HANDS-ON TIME: 23 min. **TOTAL TIME:** 38 min.

PREP TIP *The French bread dough used as the crust is quick, but it's also delicate. Carefully unroll it to prevent tearing.*

- 1 (11-ounce) can refrigerated French bread dough
- 2 teaspoons yellow cornmeal
- 1 tablespoon olive oil
- 2 cups vertically sliced onion (about 2 small)
- 1 (8-ounce) package presliced cremini mushrooms
- 3 ounces shredded white cheddar cheese (about ¾ cup)
- 6 bacon slices, cooked and coarsely crumbled
- ¼ cup finely chopped fresh flat-leaf parsley

1 **Find lengthwise seam** in dough. Beginning at seam, gently unroll dough into a rectangle on a lightly floured surface. Stretch dough into a 12-inch circle; transfer to a round pizza pan or large baking sheet sprinkled with cornmeal.

2 **Preheat oven to 425°.** Heat a large nonstick skillet over medium-high heat. Add oil to pan; swirl to coat. Add onion; sauté 8 minutes. Place onion in a bowl. Add mushrooms to pan; sauté 8 minutes or until liquid almost evaporates. Add mushrooms to onion mixture; toss.

3 **Spread onion mixture** evenly over prepared dough, leaving a ¼-inch border. Sprinkle evenly with cheese and bacon. Bake at 425° for 15 minutes or until crust is lightly browned. Sprinkle with parsley. Cut into 12 slices. Serves 6 (serving size: 2 slices)

SIMPLE SWAP *Substitute mozzarella for the white cheddar, and use any type of mushrooms you like.*

Calories 244; Fat 9.7g (sat 3.9g, mono 3.4g, poly 0.7g); Protein 11.1g; Carb 30.8g; Fiber 1.7g; Chol 20mg; Iron 2mg; Sodium 488mg; Calc 120mg

Manchego *and* Chorizo Pizza

HANDS-ON TIME: 15 min. **TOTAL TIME:** 30 min.

 PREP TIP *Slice the sausage and onion and chop the tomato while the broccoli rabe cooks.*

- ½ pound broccoli rabe (rapini), trimmed
- ⅛ teaspoon salt
- 1 (12-ounce) prebaked pizza crust
- 2 ounces shredded Manchego cheese (about ½ cup)

- 1 link Spanish chorizo sausage (about 2 ounces), thinly sliced
- ⅔ cup chopped plum tomato
- ¼ cup vertically sliced red onion

1 **Preheat oven to 450°.** Cook broccoli rabe in boiling water 4 minutes or until tender. Drain and rinse with cold water. Drain; squeeze excess moisture from broccoli rabe, and pat dry with paper towels.

2 **Coarsely chop** broccoli rabe, and sprinkle with salt.

3 **Place pizza crust** on a baking sheet. Sprinkle evenly with cheese. Top with broccoli rabe, chorizo, tomato, and onion. Bake at 450° for 12 minutes or until crust browns. Cut into 8 slices. Serves 4 (serving size: 2 slices)

Calories 382; Fat 15.4g (sat 4.7g, mono 3.7g, poly 5.6g); Protein 15.1g; Carb 46.1g; Fiber 5.1g; Chol 23mg; Iron 3.6mg; Sodium 624mg; Calc 175mg

 SIMPLE SWAP *If you can't find chorizo, substitute spicy Italian sausage—or use mild if you prefer something tamer.*

Pear *and* Prosciutto Pizza

HANDS-ON TIME: 25 min. **TOTAL TIME:** 37 min.

PREP TIP *Toasting nuts can be a delicate business since they can go from toasty to charred in seconds. To streamline prep, toast the nuts in a 350° oven—they'll take just a couple minutes. Then increase the oven temp to 450° for the pizza. It can preheat while you're cooking the onion.*

- 2 teaspoons olive oil
- 2 cups vertically sliced Oso Sweet or other sweet onion
- 1 (12-ounce) prebaked pizza crust
- 2 ounces shredded provolone cheese (about ½ cup)
- 1 medium pear, cored and thinly sliced
- 2 ounces prosciutto, cut into thin strips
- Dash of freshly ground black pepper
- 2 tablespoons chopped walnuts, toasted
- 1½ cups fresh baby arugula
- 1 teaspoon sherry vinegar

1 **Preheat oven to 450°.** Heat a large nonstick skillet over medium-high heat. Add oil to pan; swirl to coat. Add onion; cover, and cook 3 minutes. Uncover, and cook 10 minutes or until golden brown, stirring frequently.

2 **Place pizza crust** on a baking sheet. Top evenly with onion mixture; sprinkle with cheese. Top evenly with pear and prosciutto. Sprinkle with pepper. Bake at 450° for 12 minutes or until cheese melts. Sprinkle with nuts.

3 **While pizza bakes, place arugula** in a medium bowl. Drizzle vinegar over greens; toss gently to coat. Top pizza evenly with arugula mixture. Cut into 8 slices. Serves 4 (serving size: 2 slices)

SIMPLE SWAP *Arugula adds a delicious peppery bite to this pizza, but you could also use fresh baby spinach.*

Calories 446; Fat 18.8g (sat 4.9g, mono 5.1g, poly 7.3g); Protein 16.6g; Carb 55.5g; Fiber 3.8g; Chol 17mg; Iron 3.6mg; Sodium 664mg; Calc 221mg

SIMPLE SWAP

Bacon or prosciutto would be delicious variations.

138

Grilled Ham *and* Pineapple Pizza

HANDS-ON TIME: 20 min. **TOTAL TIME:** 34 min.

PREP TIP *Grilling the ham gives it a nice smoky flavor. Purchase pre-sliced pineapple from the produce section. You can also prepare this indoors on a grill pan. You may have to cook the ham and pineapple in batches, depending on the size of your pan.*

- 2 (½-inch-thick) slices fresh pineapple
- 3 ounces thinly sliced lower-sodium ham
- Cooking spray
- ½ cup spicy tomato and basil pasta sauce
- 1 (8-ounce) prebaked thin pizza crust
- 2 ounces shredded part-skim mozzarella cheese (about ½ cup)

1 **Preheat grill** to medium-high heat. Arrange pineapple and ham slices on grill rack coated with cooking spray. Grill ham 1 minute, turning once. Remove ham from grill.

2 **Grill pineapple** 9 minutes, turning once. Remove from grill; coarsely chop pineapple.

3 **Spread sauce evenly** over crust, leaving a ½-inch border; top evenly with cheese. Arrange pineapple and ham over cheese. Place pizza on grill rack coated with cooking spray; grill 7 minutes or until cheese melts. Cut into 8 slices. Serves 4 (serving size: 2 slices)

Calories 292; Fat 9.6g (sat 2.7g, mono 2.1g, poly 3.3g); Protein 12.7g; Carb 38.5g; Fiber 2.9g; Chol 17mg; Iron 2.1mg; Sodium 575mg; Calc 150mg

Peach, Gorgonzola, *and* Chicken Pizza *with* Arugula Salad

HANDS-ON TIME: 15 min. **TOTAL TIME:** 20 min.

 PREP TIP *A tangy balsamic reduction balances the sweetness of the peaches. Find fragrant peaches that yield slightly to the touch.*

- 1 (10-ounce) prebaked thin pizza crust
- Cooking spray
- 4 teaspoons extra-virgin olive oil, divided
- 2 ounces shredded part-skim mozzarella cheese (about ½ cup), divided
- 1 cup shredded cooked chicken breast
- 1½ ounces crumbled Gorgonzola cheese (about ⅓ cup)
- 1 medium peach, halved, pitted, and thinly sliced
- 1 teaspoon minced shallots
- 2 teaspoons fresh lemon juice
- ½ teaspoon honey
- 4 cups loosely packed fresh baby arugula
- ⅓ cup vertically sliced red onion
- ⅓ cup balsamic vinegar

1 **Preheat oven to 400°.** Place pizza crust on a baking sheet coated with cooking spray. Brush 1 teaspoon oil evenly over crust. Top evenly with ¼ cup mozzarella, chicken, Gorgonzola, and peach slices. Top with ¼ cup mozzarella. Bake at 400° for 11 minutes or until crust browns.

2 **While pizza bakes, combine shallots,** lemon juice, and honey in a large bowl. Gradually add 1 tablespoon oil, stirring constantly with a whisk. Add arugula and onion to bowl; toss gently to coat.

3 **Place vinegar** in a small saucepan over medium-high heat; cook 5 minutes or until reduced to 2 tablespoons. Top pizza with arugula mixture; drizzle vinegar reduction evenly over pizza. Cut into 8 slices. Serves 4 (serving size: 2 slices)

Calories 439; Fat 16.4g (sat 5.4g, mono 4.4g, poly 0.9g); Protein 25.2g; Carb 47.5g; Fiber 2.6g; Chol 47mg; Iron 3.1mg; Sodium 679mg; Calc 300mg

BBQ Chicken *and* Blue Cheese Pizza

HANDS-ON TIME: 10 min. **TOTAL TIME:** 20 min.

 PREP TIP *Round out this meal with a quick romaine salad. While the pizza bakes, toss packaged pre-cut romaine with your favorite dressing.*

- 1 (8-ounce) prebaked thin pizza crust
- ⅓ cup barbecue sauce
- 1½ cups shredded skinless, boneless rotisserie chicken breast
- ½ cup vertically sliced red onion
- ½ cup coarsely chopped yellow bell pepper
- 2 ounces crumbled blue cheese (about ½ cup)
- 2 plum tomatoes, thinly sliced (about ¼ pound)

1 **Preheat oven to 500°.** Place pizza crust on a baking sheet.

2 **Spread sauce over crust,** leaving a ½-inch border. Top evenly with chicken and remaining ingredients.

3 **Bake at 500°** for 10 minutes or until cheese melts and crust is crisp. Cut into 8 slices. Serves 4 (serving size: 2 slices)

 SIMPLE SWAP *For a kid-friendly pie, substitute fresh mozzarella for the blue cheese.*

Calories 364; Fat 11.9g (sat 4.2g, mono 3.2g, poly 4g); Protein 24.9g; Carb 39g; Fiber 2g; Chol 55mg; Iron 2.7mg; Sodium 601mg; Calc 145mg

Cheesy Chicken Bagel Pizzas

HANDS-ON TIME: 15 min. **TOTAL TIME:** 15 min.

PREP TIP *These are just as good without the chicken. Serve with a simple romaine salad tossed together while the bagels cook or Lemon-Parmesan Broccoli (page 202), which you'll need to start before you prep the pizzas.*

2 (4½-inch, 2¼-ounce) plain bagels, sliced in half

½ cup lower-sodium marinara sauce

1 cup shredded skinless, boneless rotisserie chicken breast

4 ounces preshredded part-skim mozzarella cheese (about 1 cup)

1 **Preheat broiler.** Place bagel halves, cut sides up, on a baking sheet. Broil 2 minutes or until lightly toasted.

2 **Spread 2 tablespoons** marinara on cut side of each bagel half. Top each half with ¼ cup chicken, and sprinkle with ¼ cup cheese.

3 **Broil bagel** halves an additional 2 minutes or until cheese melts. Serves 4 (serving size: 1 bagel pizza)

SIMPLE SWAP *Add sautéed spinach or roasted vegetables, substitute mushrooms for the chicken for a vegetarian option, or replace the chicken with cooked sausage or prosciutto. Since the time under the broiler is so brief, be sure to cook the toppings first.*

Calories 268; Fat 8g (sat 4.2g, mono 2.4g, poly 0.6g); Protein 22.1g; Carb 32.7g; Fiber 1g; Chol 47mg; Iron 2.9mg; Sodium 516mg; Calc 251mg

Chicken Sausage, Sweet Onion, *and* Fennel Pizza

HANDS-ON TIME: 20 min. **TOTAL TIME:** 40 min.

 PREP TIP *Serve with a salad of fresh baby spinach leaves and 1 cup halved grape tomatoes tossed with balsamic vinaigrette. Make the salad while the pizza bakes.*

3 ounces chicken apple sausage, chopped

2 teaspoons olive oil

1½ cups vertically sliced Oso Sweet or other sweet onion

1 cup thinly sliced fennel bulb (about 1 small bulb)

¼ teaspoon salt

1 (12-ounce) prebaked pizza crust

3 ounces shredded Gouda cheese (about ¾ cup)

1 tablespoon chopped fresh chives

1 **Preheat oven to 450°.** Heat a large nonstick skillet over medium-high heat. Add sausage to pan; sauté 4 minutes or until browned. Remove from pan. Add oil to pan; swirl to coat. Add onion, fennel, and salt; cover and cook 10 minutes or until tender and lightly browned.

2 **Place pizza crust** on a baking sheet. Top evenly with onion mixture; sprinkle with cheese, and top evenly with sausage.

3 **Bake at 450°** for 12 minutes or until cheese melts. Sprinkle evenly with chives. Cut into 8 slices. Serves 4 (serving size: 2 slices)

 SIMPLE SWAP *Use whatever flavor chicken or turkey sausage you prefer. Italian-, sun-dried tomato-, or pesto-flavored would all be good choices.*

Calories 420; Fat 18.9g (sat 6.1g, mono 5.4g, poly 5.6g); Protein 16g; Carb 48.4g; Fiber 3.4g; Chol 40mg; Iron 3.4mg; Sodium 642mg; Calc 248mg

Sausage, Fennel, *and* Ricotta Pizza

HANDS-ON TIME: 20 min. **TOTAL TIME:** 31 min.

SIMPLE SWAP *Skip the crushed red pepper for a milder pizza. Swap in 3 cups wilted baby spinach leaves for the fennel.*

 PREP TIP *A preheated pizza stone or baking sheet ensures an extra-crisp crust. Serve with a simple side salad.*

12 ounces refrigerated fresh pizza dough
1 (4-ounce) link turkey Italian sausage
1 cup thinly sliced fennel bulb (about 1 small bulb)
1 tablespoon yellow cornmeal
1 tablespoon extra-virgin olive oil
⅓ cup part-skim ricotta cheese

1 teaspoon minced fresh garlic
⅓ cup thinly sliced red onion
2 teaspoons fennel seeds
½ teaspoon crushed red pepper
½ teaspoon freshly ground black pepper
⅛ teaspoon kosher salt

1 **Place a pizza stone** or heavy baking sheet in oven. Preheat oven to 500° (keep pizza stone or baking sheet in oven as it preheats). Let pizza dough stand at room temperature, covered, while oven preheats.

2 **Heat a large nonstick skillet** over medium-high heat. Remove casing from sausage. Add sausage to pan; cook 4 minutes or until lightly browned, stirring to crumble. Add fennel bulb; cook 4 minutes or until tender.

3 **Roll pizza dough** into a 16-inch oval on a lightly floured surface. Carefully remove pizza stone from oven. Sprinkle cornmeal over pizza stone; place dough on pizza stone. Brush dough with oil. Sprinkle sausage mixture over dough, leaving a 1-inch border. Combine ricotta and garlic in a small bowl; top pizza with teaspoonfuls of ricotta mixture. Sprinkle onion and remaining ingredients over pizza. Bake at 500° for 11 minutes or until golden. Cut into 8 slices. Serves 4 (serving size: 2 slices)

Calories 344; Fat 9.9g (sat 2.1g, mono 4.7g, poly 1.5g); Protein 15.5g; Carb 46.4g; Fiber 7.6g; Chol 23mg; Iron 2.2mg; Sodium 646mg; Calc 84mg

Pizza Supreme

HANDS-ON TIME: 21 min. **TOTAL TIME:** 36 min.

 PREP TIP *This lightened version of a takeout favorite ups the veggies and scales back the sausage, using enough for flavor without all the grease to blot. We used full-fat mozzarella, which makes this pizza irresistible.*

- 1 pound refrigerated fresh pizza crust dough
- Cooking spray
- 2 teaspoons olive oil
- 1 (4-ounce) turkey Italian sausage link
- 1 cup sliced mushrooms
- 1 cup thinly sliced red bell pepper
- 1 cup thinly sliced orange bell pepper

- 1 cup thinly sliced onion
- ¼ teaspoon crushed red pepper
- 3 garlic cloves, thinly sliced
- ¾ cup lower-sodium marinara sauce
- 4 ounces fresh mozzarella cheese, thinly sliced

1 **Preheat oven to 500°.** Roll dough into a 14-inch circle on a lightly floured surface. Place dough on a 14-inch pizza pan or baking sheet coated with cooking spray.

2 **Heat a large nonstick skillet** over medium-high heat. Add oil to pan; swirl to coat. Remove casing from sausage. Add sausage to pan; cook 2 minutes, stirring to crumble. Add mushrooms, bell peppers, onion, crushed red pepper, and garlic; sauté 4 minutes, stirring occasionally.

3 **Spread sauce** over dough, leaving a 1-inch border. Arrange cheese evenly over sauce. Arrange turkey mixture evenly over cheese. Bake at 500° for 15 minutes or until crust and cheese are browned. Cut into 12 slices. Serves 6 (serving size: 2 slices)

SIMPLE SWAP *The two different colors of bell peppers brighten this homemade pizza, but use any combination you have on hand. Substitute hot Italian turkey sausage, if you like.*

Calories 320; Fat 9.5g (sat 3.4g, mono 4g, poly 1.1g); Protein 13.7g; Carb 48.7g; Fiber 6.5g; Chol 27mg; Iron 1.4mg; Sodium 497mg; Calc 13mg

SIMPLE SWAP *Reduced-fat Gruyère cheese will also work beautifully. Make sandwiches with sliced turkey breast instead of ham.*

Cheesy Potato Soup *with* Mini Ham Sandwiches

HANDS-ON TIME: 27 min. **TOTAL TIME:** 37 min.

 PREP TIP
To keep the texture silky smooth, stir in the cheese and remove from the heat as soon as it melts to prevent curdling.

- 1 tablespoon butter
- 1 cup chopped onion
- 2½ tablespoons all-purpose flour
- 3 cups chopped red potato (about 1 pound)
- 1¼ cups 1% low-fat milk
- ¾ cup fat-free, lower-sodium chicken broth
- ½ cup water
- 2 ounces reduced-fat shredded sharp cheddar cheese (about ½ cup)
- ⅛ teaspoon ground red pepper
- 1 tablespoon minced fresh chives
- 2 tablespoons canola mayonnaise
- 1 teaspoon Dijon mustard
- 8 (1-ounce) Hawaiian rolls, cut in half horizontally
- 4 ounces thinly sliced reduced-sodium ham
- 2 tablespoons chopped green onions

1 Preheat oven to 400°. Melt butter in a medium saucepan over medium-high heat. Add onion to pan; sauté 5 minutes or until onion is tender. Sprinkle with flour; cook 1 minute, stirring constantly.

2 Add potato, milk, broth, and ½ cup water to pan; bring to a boil. Cover, reduce heat, and simmer 10 minutes. Add cheese and pepper; cook 2 minutes or until cheese melts, stirring frequently.

3 While soup simmers, combine chives, mayonnaise, and mustard. Place rolls, cut sides up, on a baking sheet; bake at 400° for 5 minutes or until golden. Spread mayonnaise mixture on cut sides. Divide ham among roll bottoms; cover with tops. Serve with soup. Top each serving with green onions. Serves 4 (serving size: 1 cup soup, 1½ teaspoons onions, and 2 sandwiches)

Calories 514; Fat 15.9g (sat 7.6g, mono 4.3g, poly 1.7g); Protein 22.5g; Carb 66g; Fiber 4.6g; Chol 66mg; Iron 1.9mg; Sodium 789mg; Calc 323mg

Summer Squash *and* Corn Chowder

HANDS-ON TIME: 36 min. **TOTAL TIME:** 36 min.

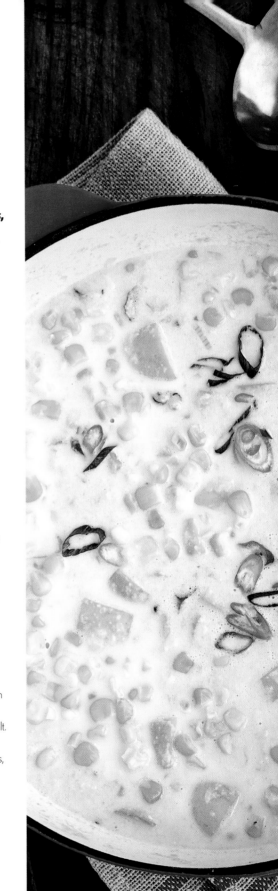

PREP TIP *Squash is the star of this soup, so choose small ones, 7 to 8 inches in length; they're sweeter and less stringy. To make a heartier chowder, add shredded cooked chicken breast. Serve with baguette toasts to dip in the soup. You can toast them while the bacon cooks.*

2 applewood-smoked bacon slices	2¼ cups 1% low-fat milk, divided
¾ cup sliced green onions, divided	1 teaspoon chopped fresh thyme
¼ cup chopped celery	⅝ teaspoon salt, divided
1 pound yellow summer squash, chopped	¼ teaspoon freshly ground black pepper
1 pound frozen white and yellow baby corn kernels, thawed and divided	1 ounce shredded extra-sharp cheddar cheese (about ¼ cup)

1 **Cook bacon** in a large Dutch oven over medium-high heat until crisp. Remove bacon from pan, reserving 2 teaspoons drippings in pan. Crumble bacon, and set aside. Add ½ cup onions, celery, and squash to drippings in pan; sauté 8 minutes or until vegetables are tender.

2 **Reserve 1 cup corn;** set aside. Place remaining corn and 1 cup milk in a blender; process until smooth. Add 1¼ cups milk, thyme, ½ teaspoon salt, and pepper to blender; process just until combined.

3 **Add pureed mixture** and reserved 1 cup corn to pan. Reduce heat to medium; cook 5 minutes or until thoroughly heated, stirring constantly. Stir in ⅛ teaspoon salt. Ladle about 1½ cups soup into each of 4 bowls; top each serving with about 1 tablespoon bacon, 1 tablespoon onions, and 1 tablespoon cheese. Serves 4

Calories 285; Fat 9.4g (sat 3.9g, mono 3.4g, poly 1.2g); Protein 13.3g; Carb 37.8g; Fiber 5.4g; Chol 20mg; Iron 1.3mg; Sodium 605mg; Calc 260mg

SIMPLE SWAP

To make this soup vegetarian, omit the bacon and add 2 teaspoons olive oil in place of the drippings.

Roasted Fennel, Tomato, *and* Chickpea Soup

HANDS-ON TIME: 15 min. **TOTAL TIME:** 60 min.

 PREP TIP *Roasting the onion and fennel gives this dish a richer, deeper flavor. Spread the vegetables in a single layer to ensure each piece cooks evenly.*

2 cups chopped fennel bulb (about 1 small bulb)
2 cups chopped onion
Cooking spray
1 (15½-ounce) can organic chickpeas (garbanzo beans), rinsed and drained
2 teaspoons butter
3 garlic cloves, minced

2 (14-ounce) cans fat-free, lower-sodium chicken broth
2 (14½-ounce) cans organic diced tomatoes, undrained
½ teaspoon freshly ground black pepper
⅛ teaspoon salt
2 (6-inch) pitas, each cut into 8 wedges

1 **Preheat oven to 425°.** Arrange fennel and onion in a single layer on a jelly-roll pan coated with cooking spray; toss to coat.

2 **Bake at 425°** for 25 minutes, stirring after 15 minutes. Add chickpeas to vegetable mixture. Bake an additional 20 minutes or until fennel is tender and chickpeas start to brown, stirring after 10 minutes.

3 **Melt butter** in a large saucepan over medium heat. Add garlic to pan, and cook 1 minute, stirring occasionally. Add vegetable mixture, broth, and next 3 ingredients (through salt) to pan; bring to a boil. Cook 3 minutes or until thoroughly heated. Remove from heat. Serve with pita wedges. Serves 4 (serving size: 2 cups soup and 4 pita wedges)

Calories 301; Fat 3.3g (sat 1.4g, mono 0.6g, poly 0.3g); Protein 12.5g; Carb 55.9g; Fiber 10.7g; Chol 5mg; Iron 3mg; Sodium 667mg; Calc 157mg

SIMPLE SWAP

You can also make this with sweet potatoes instead of butternut squash.

Butternut Squash Soup *with* Cheese Toasts

HANDS-ON TIME: 21 min. **TOTAL TIME:** 63 min.

PREP TIP *You can make this creamy soup even faster by using packaged peeled butternut squash cubes, or purchasing frozen cubes and thawing them. Serve with a baby spinach salad tossed with sliced red onion and red wine vinaigrette. Prep the salad ingredients while the soup simmers and toss together just before serving.*

1 tablespoon butter	¼ cup half-and-half
3½ cups cubed peeled butternut squash (about 1½ pounds)	⅛ teaspoon salt
	4 (1-ounce) slices French bread
¾ cup chopped carrot	3 ounces thinly sliced Swiss cheese
½ cup chopped sweet onion	Freshly ground black pepper (optional)
2½ cups fat-free, lower-sodium chicken broth	

Melt butter in a large saucepan over medium-high heat. Add squash, carrot, and onion; sauté 12 minutes. Add broth, and bring to a boil. Cover, reduce heat, and simmer 30 minutes. Remove from heat; stir in half-and-half and salt.

While soup simmers, preheat broiler. Place squash mixture in a blender. Remove center piece of blender lid (to allow steam to escape), and secure blender lid on blender. Place a clean towel over opening in blender lid (to avoid splatters). Blend until smooth.

Arrange French bread on a baking sheet. Broil 1 minute or until lightly toasted. Turn bread over, and top evenly with Swiss cheese. Broil 1 minute or until bubbly. Serve toasts with soup. Garnish with black pepper, if desired. Serves 4 (serving size: about 1 cup soup and 1 toast)

Calories 297; Fat 10.7g (sat 6.7g, mono 2.3g, poly 0.4g); Protein 11.8g; Carb 42.4g; Fiber 4.9g; Chol 33mg; Iron 2.3mg; Sodium 645mg; Calc 315mg

SIMPLE SWAP *You can substitute cod or another flaky white fish for the halibut.*

Herbed Fish *and* Red Potato Chowder

HANDS-ON TIME: 26 min. **TOTAL TIME:** 34 min.

 PREP TIP
A crusty baguette is the ideal complement to this chowder—you'll need it to soak up the flavorful broth. You can toast it while the soup finishes, if you like.

- 2 bacon slices
- 3 cups diced red potato (about 1 pound)
- 1 cup chopped onion
- 3 tablespoons all-purpose flour
- 2 (8-ounce) bottles clam juice
- 2 cups 2% reduced-fat milk
- 1 tablespoon chopped fresh thyme
- ¼ teaspoon salt
- ¼ teaspoon freshly ground black pepper
- 12 ounces skinless halibut fillets, cut into 1-inch pieces
- 2 tablespoons chopped fresh flat-leaf parsley

1 **Cook bacon** in a Dutch oven over medium-high heat until crisp. Remove bacon from pan, reserving 1 tablespoon drippings in pan. Cool bacon, and crumble; set aside.

2 **While bacon cools, add potato** and onion to drippings in pan; sauté 3 minutes or until onion is tender. Add flour to pan; cook 1 minute, stirring constantly. Stir in clam juice; bring to a boil. Cover, reduce heat, and simmer 6 minutes or until potato is tender.

3 **Stir in milk;** bring to a simmer over medium-high heat, stirring constantly (do not boil). Stir in thyme, salt, pepper, and fish; cook 3 minutes or until fish flakes easily when tested with a fork. Stir in parsley. Sprinkle evenly with bacon. Serves 4 (serving size: 2 cups)

Calories 307; Fat 8.1g (sat 3.5g, mono 3g, poly 0.9g); Protein 24.4g; Carb 33.9g; Fiber 2.5g; Chol 57mg; Iron 2.2mg; Sodium 611mg; Calc 198mg

Halibut *and* Chorizo Stew *with* Garlic Toasts

HANDS-ON TIME: 15 min. **TOTAL TIME:** 20 min.

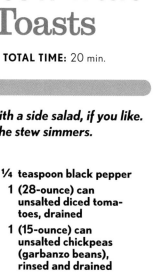

PREP TIP *Pair this hearty meal with a side salad, if you like. You can make it while the stew simmers.*

- 2 teaspoons olive oil, divided
- 2 ounces Spanish chorizo sausage, diced
- 1 cup chopped onion
- 3 garlic cloves, sliced
- ½ cup dry sherry
- ½ cup fat-free, lower-sodium chicken broth
- 1½ tablespoons chopped fresh flat-leaf parsley
- ¼ teaspoon kosher salt
- ¼ teaspoon black pepper
- 1 (28-ounce) can unsalted diced tomatoes, drained
- 1 (15-ounce) can unsalted chickpeas (garbanzo beans), rinsed and drained
- 4 (5-ounce) skinless halibut fillets
- 4 (½-ounce) slices ciabatta bread
- 1 garlic clove, halved

1 **Preheat broiler.** Heat a large sauté pan over medium heat. Add 1 teaspoon oil to pan; swirl to coat. Add chorizo, and sauté 3 minutes or until lightly browned. Add onion; sauté 3 minutes or until just tender. Add sliced garlic; sauté 1 minute. Add sherry; cook 1½ minutes, scraping pan to loosen browned bits. Stir in broth and next 5 ingredients; stir to combine.

2 **Nestle halibut fillets** in stew; spoon tomato mixture over fillets. Cover and simmer 5 minutes or until fish flakes easily when tested with a fork.

3 **Place ciabatta slices** on a baking sheet. Broil 1 minute or until toasted. Brush toasts with 1 teaspoon oil; rub toasts with cut sides of halved garlic clove. Serve toasts with stew. Serves 4 (serving size: 1 fillet, about 1¼ cups stew, and 1 toast)

Calories 422; Fat 12.4g (sat 2.9g, mono 5.8g, poly 1.8g); Protein 39.2g; Carb 31.2g; Fiber 4.8g; Chol 58mg; Iron 3.8mg; Sodium 702mg; Calc 126mg

SIMPLE SWAP *If you can't find chorizo, substitute hot turkey Italian sausage.*

Spicy Shrimp Noodle Bowl

HANDS-ON TIME: 22 min. **TOTAL TIME:** 31 min.

PREP TIP *Serve this soup with a simple side of fresh cucumber slices tossed with thinly sliced radishes, green onions, freshly ground black pepper, and your favorite vinaigrette. Prepare it while the broth mixture comes to a boil.*

- 1 pound tail-on peeled and deveined medium shrimp
- 1½ cups water
- 1 cup fat-free, lower-sodium chicken broth
- 1 (8-ounce) bottle clam juice
- 2 (¼-inch-thick) slices peeled fresh ginger
- 1 teaspoon olive oil
- ¾ cup thinly sliced red bell pepper
- ¼ cup thinly sliced yellow onion
- 1 garlic clove, minced
- ½ cup sugar snap peas, trimmed
- 2 teaspoons chili garlic sauce or ½ teaspoon crushed red pepper
- ¼ teaspoon salt
- 3 ounces uncooked wide rice sticks (rice-flour noodles)
- 2 tablespoons cilantro leaves
- 4 lime wedges

1 **Remove shrimp tails;** set shrimp aside. Combine shrimp tails, 1½ cups water, broth, clam juice, and ginger in a saucepan; bring to a boil. Reduce heat; simmer, uncovered, 10 minutes. Strain broth mixture through a sieve into a bowl; discard solids.

2 **While broth mixture simmers, heat a medium saucepan** over medium-high heat. Add oil to pan; swirl to coat. Add bell pepper, onion, and garlic; sauté 3 minutes. Add reserved broth; bring to a simmer.

3 **Add shrimp,** peas, chili garlic sauce, salt, and noodles to pan; cook 5 minutes or until noodles are done. Ladle 1¼ cups soup into each of 4 bowls; top each serving with 1½ teaspoons cilantro. Serve with lime wedges. Serves 4

Calories 236; Fat 3.6g (sat 0.7g, mono 1.3g, poly 1g); Protein 26.5g; Carb 25.4g; Fiber 1.9g; Chol 174mg; Iron 3.7mg; Sodium 506mg; Calc 84mg

Old-Fashioned Chicken Noodle Soup

HANDS-ON TIME: 10 min. **TOTAL TIME:** 46 min.

 PREP TIP *Bone-in chicken fortifies commercial stock and adds meaty depth to this classic soup.*

- 8 **cups unsalted chicken stock**
- 2 **(4-ounce) skinless, bone-in chicken thighs**
- 1 **(12-ounce) skinless, bone-in chicken breast half**
- 2 **cups diagonally cut carrot**
- 2 **cups diagonally cut celery**
- 1 **cup chopped onion**
- 6 **ounces uncooked medium egg noodles**
- ½ **teaspoon kosher salt**
- ½ **teaspoon freshly ground black pepper**
- **Celery leaves (optional)**

 1 **Combine first 3 ingredients** in a Dutch oven over medium-high heat; bring to a boil. Reduce heat; simmer 20 minutes. Remove chicken from pan; let stand 10 minutes.

 2 **While chicken stands, add carrot,** celery, and onion to pan; cover and simmer 10 minutes. Add noodles, and simmer 6 minutes.

 3 **While noodles simmer, remove chicken** from bones; shred meat into bite-sized pieces. Discard bones. Add chicken, salt, and pepper to pan; cook 2 minutes or until noodles are done. Garnish with celery leaves, if desired. Serves 4 (serving size: about 1½ cups)

 SIMPLE SWAP *You can use all chicken breast if you like, but the flavor won't be quite as rich.*

Calories 402; Fat 7g (sat 2g, mono 1.6g, poly 0.9g); Protein 39.7g; Carb 43.7g; Fiber 4.7g; Chol 137mg; Iron 3.1mg; Sodium 583mg; Calc 112mg

Mexican Chicken-Hominy Soup

HANDS-ON TIME: 18 min. **TOTAL TIME:** 28 min.

 PREP TIP *You can make this ahead. Refrigerate cooked, cooled soup up to two days. Serve with tortilla chips.*

1 tablespoon olive oil
1¾ cups chopped onion
3 garlic cloves, minced
1 jalapeño pepper, seeded and minced
2 cups shredded skinless, boneless rotisserie chicken breast
¼ teaspoon freshly ground black pepper

2 (14-ounce) cans fat-free, lower-sodium chicken broth
1 (15.5-ounce) can hominy, rinsed and drained
½ cup thinly sliced radishes
2 tablespoons cilantro leaves
4 lime wedges

1 **Heat a large saucepan** over medium-high heat. Add oil to pan; swirl to coat. Add onion; sauté 2 minutes. Stir in garlic and jalapeño; sauté 1 minute.

2 **Add chicken,** pepper, and broth; bring to a boil. Reduce heat, and simmer 5 minutes.

3 **Stir in hominy;** bring to a boil. Cook 5 minutes. Ladle about 1½ cups soup into each of 4 bowls; top each serving with 2 tablespoons radishes and 1½ teaspoons cilantro. Serve with lime wedges. Serves 4

 SIMPLE SWAP *If you can't find hominy, substitute 1 cup thawed frozen corn.*

Calories 235; Fat 6.6g (sat 1.3g, mono 3.5g, poly 1.2g); Protein 24.8g; Carb 18g; Fiber 3.3g; Chol 60mg; Iron 1.5mg; Sodium 641mg; Calc 43mg

SIMPLE SWAP *Make with leftover roast turkey instead of chicken, button mushrooms instead of an exotic blend, or quick-cooking white or brown rice instead of wild rice.*

Wild Rice *and* Mushroom Soup *with* Chicken

HANDS-ON TIME: 13 min. **TOTAL TIME:** 17 min.

PREP TIP *To save time, use packaged matchstick-cut carrots. Add sliced whole-wheat French bread and mixed salad greens tossed with your favorite dressing to complete the menu. You can make the salad while the soup heats.*

4 cups fat-free, lower-sodium chicken broth, divided

1 (2¾-ounce) package quick-cooking wild rice

1 tablespoon olive oil

½ cup prechopped onion

½ cup chopped red bell pepper

⅓ cup matchstick-cut carrots

1 teaspoon minced fresh garlic

½ teaspoon dried thyme

1 teaspoon butter

2 (4-ounce) packages presliced exotic mushroom blend (such as shiitake, cremini, and oyster)

2 cups shredded cooked chicken breast

⅛ teaspoon salt

⅛ teaspoon freshly ground black pepper

1 **Bring 1⅓ cups** broth to a boil in a medium saucepan; add rice to pan. Cover, reduce heat, and simmer 5 minutes or until liquid is absorbed. Set aside.

2 **While rice cooks, heat a Dutch oven** over medium-high heat. Add oil to pan; swirl to coat. Add onion and next 4 ingredients (through thyme) to pan; sauté 3 minutes, stirring occasionally. Stir in butter and mushrooms; sauté 3 minutes or until lightly browned.

3 **Add remaining 2⅔ cups broth,** rice, chicken, salt, and pepper to pan; cook 3 minutes or until thoroughly heated, stirring occasionally. Serves 4 (serving size: 1½ cups)

Calories 281; Fat 7.5g (sat 1.9g, mono 3.8g, poly 1.3g); Protein 28.9g; Carb 23g; Fiber 4g; Chol 62mg; Iron 2.8mg; Sodium 541mg; Calc 42mg

SIMPLE SWAP *Use regular chili powder in place of ancho and decrease the cumin by half.*

Ancho Pork *and* Hominy Stew

HANDS-ON TIME: 24 min. **TOTAL TIME:** 49 min.

 You can freeze the stew for up to two months. Serve with corn bread. Prepare the bread first so it can bake while you make the stew.

- 2 tablespoons ancho chile powder
- 2 teaspoons dried oregano
- 1½ teaspoons Spanish smoked paprika
- 1 teaspoon ground cumin
- ½ teaspoon salt
- 1½ pounds pork tenderloin, trimmed and cut into ½-inch pieces
- 1 tablespoon olive oil, divided
- 2 cups chopped onion
- 1½ cups chopped green bell pepper
- 1 tablespoon minced fresh garlic
- 2½ cups fat-free, lower-sodium chicken broth
- 1 (28-ounce) can hominy, drained
- 1 (14½-ounce) can fire-roasted diced tomatoes, undrained

1 Combine first 5 ingredients in a large bowl; set 1½ teaspoons spice mixture aside. Add pork to remaining spice mixture in bowl, tossing well to coat.

2 Heat a large Dutch oven over medium-high heat. Add 2 teaspoons oil to pan; swirl to coat. Add pork mixture; cook 5 minutes or until browned, stirring occasionally. Remove pork from pan; set aside.

3 Add 1 teaspoon oil to pan. Add onion, bell pepper, and garlic; sauté 5 minutes or until tender. Return pork to pan. Add reserved 1½ teaspoons spice mixture, broth, hominy, and tomatoes; bring to a boil. Partially cover, reduce heat, and simmer 25 minutes. Serves 6 (serving size: 1⅓ cups)

Calories 300; Fat 8.3g (sat 2.1g, mono 3.7g, poly 1.4g); Protein 28.9g; Carb 26.9g; Fiber 6.1g; Chol 76mg; Iron 3.2mg; Sodium 523mg; Calc 51mg

Pinto Bean Slow-Cooker Chili

HANDS-ON TIME: 20 min. **TOTAL TIME:** 8 hr. 20 min.

 PREP TIP *You can assemble this in the slow cooker insert the night before, cover, and refrigerate it overnight. All you'll need to do the next morning is pop the insert into the cooker and turn it on. Save even more time by using prechopped onion.*

1 tablespoon olive oil
1½ cups chopped onion
1½ cups chopped red bell pepper
1 garlic clove, minced
2 tablespoons chili powder
½ teaspoon ground cumin
2 (12-ounce) packages cubed peeled butternut squash (about 5¼ cups)
3 cups cooked pinto beans

1½ cups water
1 cup frozen whole-kernel corn
1 teaspoon salt
1 (14½-ounce) can crushed tomatoes, undrained
1 (4½-ounce) can chopped green chiles, undrained
3 ounces crumbled queso fresco (about ¾ cup)
6 lime wedges

 1 **Heat a large nonstick skillet** over medium heat. Add oil to pan; swirl to coat. Add onion, bell pepper, and garlic; cover and cook 5 minutes or until tender. Add chili powder and cumin; cook 1 minute, stirring constantly.

 2 **Place onion mixture** in a 5-quart electric slow cooker. Add squash and next 6 ingredients (through chiles).

 3 **Cover and cook** on LOW 8 hours or until vegetables are tender and chili is thick. Sprinkle with cheese; serve with lime wedges. Serves 6 (serving size: 1½ cups chili, 2 tablespoons cheese, and 1 lime wedge)

Calories 320; Fat 5.9g (sat 2.1g, mono 2.6g, poly 0.7g); Protein 15.3g; Carb 55.7g; Fiber 13.6g; Chol 10mg; Iron 4mg; Sodium 650mg; Calc 224mg

Chicken *and* Barley Stew

HANDS-ON TIME: 17 min. **TOTAL TIME:** 17 min.

 PREP TIP *This stew comes together quickly, but use prechopped onion to make it even quicker to prepare. Serve with crackers.*

1 cup uncooked quick-cooking barley

3 (14-ounce) cans fat-free, lower-sodium chicken broth

1 tablespoon olive oil

1¾ cups chopped onion

1 (10-ounce) package frozen mixed vegetables

1 cup chopped cooked chicken

¼ teaspoon dried thyme

¼ teaspoon freshly ground black pepper

1 **Bring barley and broth** to a boil in a large saucepan. Reduce heat, and simmer 5 minutes.

2 **While barley cooks, heat a large nonstick skillet** over medium-high heat. Add oil to pan; swirl to coat. Add onion; sauté 3 minutes.

3 **Add mixed vegetables;** sauté 2 minutes. Add vegetable mixture, chicken, thyme, and pepper to barley mixture; simmer 4 minutes. Serves 4 (serving size: about 1¾ cups)

 SIMPLE SWAP *Make with quick-cooking rice instead of barley and your choice of frozen vegetables.*

 SIMPLE SWAP *Queso fresco is a crumbly, slightly salty Mexican cheese that's available in many large supermarkets. If you can't find it, substitute crumbled feta.*

Calories 356; Fat 7.5g (sat 1.5g, mono 1.9g, poly 3.3g); Protein 22.7g; Carb 50.7g; Fiber 12.1g; Chol 31mg; Iron 3.1mg; Sodium 618mg; Calc 54mg

Green Chile Chili

HANDS-ON TIME: 20 min. **TOTAL TIME:** 65 min.

PREP TIP

Serve this tangy chili with corn bread or corn muffins from a packaged mix. Put them in the oven to bake while the chili simmers. Or, serve the chili over baked potatoes—pierce 4 medium baking potatoes with a sharp knife, and bake at 400° for 1 hour or until potatoes are soft when squeezed. Put them in to bake before you start the chili.

SIMPLE SWAP *Make with ground turkey or chicken instead of beef.*

1 tablespoon canola oil
12 ounces ground sirloin
1½ cups chopped onion
1 tablespoon chili powder
1 teaspoon hot paprika
5 garlic cloves, minced
1 (12-ounce) bottle dark beer
½ cup salsa verde
1 (4-ounce) can diced green chiles, undrained

1 (15-ounce) can unsalted tomatoes, undrained and crushed
1 (15-ounce) can organic kidney beans, rinsed and drained
1 ounce shredded sharp cheddar cheese (about ¼ cup)
1 green onion, sliced

1 **Heat a large Dutch oven** over medium-high heat. Add oil to pan; swirl to coat. Add beef; sauté 5 minutes or until no longer pink, stirring to crumble.

2 **Add chopped onion,** chili powder, and paprika; cook 4 minutes, stirring occasionally. Add garlic; sauté 1 minute.

3 **Stir in beer;** bring to a boil. Cook 15 minutes or until liquid almost evaporates. Add salsa and next 3 ingredients (through beans); bring to a boil. Reduce heat; simmer 30 minutes, stirring occasionally. Ladle 1¼ cups chili into each of 4 bowls; top each serving with 1 tablespoon cheese. Sprinkle evenly with green onions. Serves 4

Calories 310; Fat 10.6g (sat 3.3g, mono 1.5g, poly 4.4g); Protein 24.1g; Carb 25.1g; Fiber 4.3g; Chol 52mg; Iron 4.8mg; Sodium 575mg; Calc 95mg

Three-Bean Chili

HANDS-ON TIME: 21 min. **TOTAL TIME:** 1 hr. 31 min.

 PREP TIP *This is an excellent make-ahead option that stores well. Decrease (or omit) the crushed red pepper if you want a milder chili.*

2 red bell peppers

3 tablespoons extra-virgin olive oil

1 cup chopped onion

2 teaspoons ground cumin

1 teaspoon crushed red pepper

1 teaspoon paprika

⅛ teaspoon salt

4 garlic cloves, thinly sliced

2 cups organic vegetable broth

1½ cups (½-inch) cubed peeled butternut squash

1 (28-ounce) can unsalted tomatoes, undrained and chopped

1 (15-ounce) can pinto beans, rinsed and drained

1 (15-ounce) can cannellini beans, rinsed and drained

1 (15-ounce) can red kidney beans, rinsed and drained

½ cup thinly sliced green onions

1 **Preheat broiler.** Cut bell peppers in half lengthwise. Remove and discard seeds and membranes. Place pepper halves, skin sides up, on a foil-lined baking sheet. Broil 15 minutes or until blackened. Place pepper halves in a zip-top plastic bag; seal. Let stand 15 minutes.

2 **While peppers stand, heat a Dutch oven** over medium-low heat. Add oil to pan; swirl to coat. Add onion; cook 15 minutes, stirring occasionally. Stir in cumin and next 4 ingredients (through garlic); cook 2 minutes, stirring frequently.

3 **Peel and chop peppers.** Add bell peppers, broth, squash, and tomatoes to pan; bring to a simmer. Cook 20 minutes, stirring occasionally. Add beans; simmer 25 minutes or until slightly thick, stirring occasionally. Sprinkle with green onions. Serves 6 (serving size: about 1½ cups)

Calories 264; Fat 8.3g (sat 1.2g, mono 5.2g, poly 1.3g); Protein 9.5g; Carb 40.9g; Fiber 10.7g; Chol 0mg; Iron 4.4mg; Sodium 641mg; Calc 145mg

Fast Chicken Chili

HANDS-ON TIME: 23 min. **TOTAL TIME:** 23 min.

 This chili has a tad bit of a kick that pairs nicely with a topping of cooling sliced avocado. Slice the avocado and sprinkle with fresh lime juice to preserve the color.

- 1 tablespoon canola oil
- 1 pound skinless, boneless chicken breast, cut into bite-sized pieces
- ¾ teaspoon salt, divided
- ½ cup vertically sliced onion
- 2 teaspoons minced fresh garlic
- 2 teaspoons ground cumin
- 1 teaspoon ground coriander
- ½ teaspoon dried oregano
- ¼ teaspoon ground red pepper
- 3 cups unsalted canned cannellini beans, rinsed, drained, and divided
- 1 cup water
- 2 (4-ounce) cans chopped green chiles, undrained and divided
- 1 (14-ounce) can fat-free, lower-sodium chicken broth
- ¼ cup cilantro leaves
- 6 lime wedges

1 **Heat a Dutch oven** over medium-high heat. Add oil to pan; swirl to coat. Sprinkle chicken with ¼ teaspoon salt. Add chicken to pan; sauté 4 minutes.

2 **Add onion** and next 5 ingredients (through red pepper); sauté 3 minutes. Add 2 cups beans, 1 cup water, ½ teaspoon salt, 1 can chiles, and broth to pan; bring to a boil.

3 **Mash remaining beans** and remaining chiles in a bowl. Add to chili; simmer 5 minutes. Serve with cilantro and lime wedges. Serves 6 (serving size: 1 cup chili, 2 teaspoons cilantro, and 1 lime wedge)

Calories 189; Fat 4.3g (sat 0.5g, mono 1.8g, poly 1g); Protein 22.3g; Carb 15.1g; Fiber 4.8g; Chol 44mg; Iron 2.6mg; Sodium 624mg; Calc 67mg

  SIMPLE SWAP *Substitute ground turkey or ground sirloin in place of chicken.*

Goat Cheese *and* Roasted Corn Quesadillas

HANDS-ON TIME: 15 min. **TOTAL TIME:** 15 min.

 PREP TIP *Browning the corn caramelizes its sugars and deepens the taste of the quesadillas. Serve with black beans. Heat them in a small saucepan over medium heat for 5 minutes or until heated. Put them on to warm before starting the quesadillas.*

2 teaspoons canola oil
1 cup fresh corn kernels (about 1 large ear)
5 ounces softened goat cheese (about ⅔ cup)
8 (6-inch) corn tortillas

¼ cup chopped green onions (about 1 green onion)
10 tablespoons salsa verde, divided
Cooking spray

1 **Heat a large skillet** over medium-high heat. Add oil to pan; swirl to coat. Add corn; sauté 2 minutes or until browned. Place corn in a bowl. Add cheese to corn; stir until well blended. Divide corn mixture among 4 tortillas; spread to within ¼ inch of sides. Sprinkle each tortilla with 1 tablespoon onions. Top each with 1½ teaspoons salsa and remaining tortillas.

2 **Heat pan** over medium-high heat. Coat pan with cooking spray. Place 2 quesadillas in pan; cook 1½ minutes on each side or until golden. Remove from pan; keep warm.

3 **Wipe pan clean** with paper towels; recoat pan with cooking spray. Repeat procedure with remaining quesadillas. Cut each quesadilla into 4 wedges. Serve with remaining salsa. Serves 4 (serving size: 4 wedges and 2 tablespoons salsa)

Calories 244; Fat 12.3g (sat 5.4g, mono 3.3g, poly 1.6g); Protein 9.9g; Carb 28.6g; Fiber 3.2g; Chol 16mg; Iron 1mg; Sodium 266mg; Calc 75mg

Arctic Char Sandwiches *with* Lemon-Tarragon Slaw

HANDS-ON TIME: 15 min. **TOTAL TIME:** 15 min.

 PREP TIP *Canola mayo has less saturated fat than regular. Tarragon adds a light licorice flavor.*

- 1 tablespoon olive oil
- ½ teaspoon freshly ground black pepper, divided
- ³/₈ teaspoon salt, divided
- 4 (4-ounce) arctic char fillets
- 1¼ cups cabbage-and-carrot coleslaw
- 1 tablespoon chopped fresh tarragon
- 2 tablespoons canola mayonnaise
- 1 tablespoon fresh lemon juice
- 1 teaspoon Dijon mustard
- 4 (2-ounce) Kaiser rolls, toasted

1 Heat a large nonstick skillet over medium-high heat. Add oil to pan; swirl to coat. Sprinkle ¼ teaspoon pepper and ¼ teaspoon salt evenly over both sides of fish. Add fish to pan; cook 4 minutes on each side or until fish flakes easily when tested with a fork or until desired degree of doneness.

2 Combine coleslaw, ¼ teaspoon pepper, ⅛ teaspoon salt, tarragon, mayonnaise, lemon juice, and mustard; toss well.

3 Arrange 1 fillet over bottom half of each roll; top with ¼ cup slaw and top half of roll. Serves 4 (serving size: 1 sandwich)

Calories 406; Fat 18.4g (sat 2.7g, mono 7.9g, poly 6.5g); Protein 26.7g; Carb 32g; Fiber 1.9g; Chol 56mg; Iron 2.4mg; Sodium 655mg; Calc 77mg

Open-Faced Blackened Catfish Sandwiches

HANDS-ON TIME: 20 min. **TOTAL TIME:** 25 min.

PREP TIP *You can chop the tender tops of cilantro stems right along with the leaves. Serve with Stewed Okra and Fresh Tomato (page 207). You can prepare the sandwiches while the side simmers.*

- 1¾ teaspoons paprika
- 1 teaspoon dried oregano
- ¾ teaspoon ground red pepper
- ¼ teaspoon salt
- ¼ teaspoon freshly ground black pepper
- 4 (6-ounce) catfish fillets
- 2 teaspoons olive oil
- ⅓ cup plain fat-free Greek yogurt

- 3 tablespoons fresh lime juice
- 1 tablespoon honey
- 2 cups packaged cabbage-and-carrot coleslaw
- 1 cup chopped fresh cilantro
- 4 (1-ounce) slices sourdough bread, toasted

1 **Combine first 5 ingredients** in a small bowl. Sprinkle both sides of fish with paprika mixture. Heat a large cast-iron skillet over high heat. Add oil to pan; swirl to coat. Add fish; cook 4 minutes on each side or until fish flakes easily when tested with a fork.

2 **While fish cooks, combine yogurt,** juice, and honey in a medium bowl. Add coleslaw and cilantro; toss well to coat.

3 **Top each bread slice** with about ½ cup slaw and 1 fillet. Top each fillet with remaining slaw. Serves 4 (serving size: 1 open-faced sandwich)

SIMPLE SWAP *Arctic char can sometimes be hard to find out of season; feel free to use salmon instead.*

Calories 362; Fat 16g (sat 3.4g, mono 7.8g, poly 3.2g); Protein 31.3g; Carb 22.6g; Fiber 2.2g; Chol 80mg; Iron 2.4mg; Sodium 414mg; Calc 63mg

Shrimp Salad Rolls

HANDS-ON TIME: 15 min. **TOTAL TIME:** 25 min.

 Citrus and herbs give this shrimp salad brightness and tang. Serve with roasted potatoes. You can purchase refrigerated potato wedges, which can cook while you prepare the shrimp salad.

1 tablespoon butter
20 large shrimp, peeled and deveined (about 1 pound)
¼ cup canola mayonnaise
1 teaspoon grated lemon rind
1 tablespoon fresh lemon juice
2 tablepoons chopped fresh parsley

1½ teaspoons chopped fresh tarragon
½ teaspoon freshly ground black pepper
¼ teaspoon kosher salt
4 (1½-ounce) hot dog buns
8 Boston lettuce leaves

1 Preheat broiler. Heat butter in a large nonstick skillet over medium-high heat; swirl to coat. Add shrimp to pan; sauté 4 minutes or until done. Place shrimp on a large plate; chill in refrigerator 10 minutes.

2 Coarsely chop shrimp. Combine chopped shrimp, mayonnaise, and next 6 ingredients (through salt) in a large bowl.

3 Open buns without completely splitting; arrange, cut sides up, on a baking sheet. Broil 1 minute or until toasted. Place 2 lettuce leaves in each bun; top each serving with ½ cup shrimp mixture. Serves 4 (serving size: 1 sandwich)

Calories 370; Fat 17.8g (sat 3.7g, mono 7.5g, poly 4.7g); Protein 27.4g; Carb 23g; Fiber 1.2g; Chol 185mg; Iron 4.4mg; Sodium 616mg; Calc 128mg

 SIMPLE SWAP *Vary the herbs in the shrimp salad or serve on any variety of toasted bread you have on hand.*

Tuna Salad Melt

HANDS-ON TIME: 15 min. **TOTAL TIME:** 15 min.

PREP TIP *The walnuts and chickpeas elevate this classic sandwich, giving it an untraditional texture and flavor that pair wonderfully with nutty Swiss cheese. Serve with a simple spinach salad or baked sweet potato fries. Bake the fries first, and then preheat the broiler to melt the cheese on the sandwiches.*

¼ cup chopped walnuts
¼ cup chopped red onion
¼ cup canned chickpeas (garbanzo beans), rinsed and drained
¼ cup canola mayonnaise
1 tablespoon Dijon mustard
1 teaspoon red wine vinegar
¼ teaspoon hot pepper sauce
½ teaspoon salt

½ teaspoon freshly ground black pepper
1 (12-ounce) can solid white tuna in water, drained and flaked
1 garlic clove, minced
6 (1-ounce) slices multigrain bread
1½ ounces shredded Swiss cheese (about ⅓ cup)
12 (¼-inch-thick) slices tomato
1 cup fresh baby spinach

1 **Preheat broiler.** Combine first 11 ingredients in a medium bowl; toss gently.

2 **Top bread** evenly with cheese; broil 4 minutes or until bubbly.

3 **Arrange 2 tomato slices** and about ⅓ cup tuna mixture over each bread slice. Top sandwiches evenly with spinach. Serves 6 (serving size: 1 open-faced sandwich)

Calories 231; Fat 11.1g (sat 1.9g, mono 2.9g, poly 3.8g); Protein 15.2g; Carb 18g; Fiber 3.9g; Chol 21mg; Iron 1.4mg; Sodium 500mg; Calc 94mg

Roast Beef Sandwiches *with* Watercress Slaw

HANDS-ON TIME: 8 min. **TOTAL TIME:** 8 min.

PREP TIP *Start with deli roast beef and a package of angel hair slaw to create a hearty sandwich that's perfect for a quick no-cook dinner. Let the butter soften for 15 minutes to make spreading it easier.*

1 cup packaged angel hair slaw

1 cup chopped trimmed watercress

⅓ cup thinly sliced green onions

2 tablespoons minced fresh tarragon

3 tablespoons canola mayonnaise

¼ teaspoon freshly ground black pepper

1 (8-ounce) French bread baguette

4 teaspoons butter, softened

8 ounces thinly sliced lower-sodium, deli roast beef

8 (¼-inch-thick) slices tomato

1 **Combine first 6 ingredients** in a medium bowl, tossing gently.

2 **Cut baguette crosswise** into 4 pieces. Cut each piece in half horizontally using a serrated knife.

3 **Spread 1 teaspoon butter** on each bottom half of baguette. Divide roast beef evenly over bottom halves of baguette. Arrange 2 tomato slices, and about 1 cup slaw mixture over each sandwich; top with top halves of baguette. Serves 4 (serving size: 1 sandwich)

Calories 358; Fat 14.8g (sat 4.2g, mono 6.5g, poly 2.4g); Protein 21.3g; Carb 37.5g; Fiber 2.2g; Chol 44mg; Iron 3.7mg; Sodium 585mg; Calc 26mg

 SIMPLE SWAP *Watercress adds a peppery bite to this sandwich. If you can't find it, use arugula instead. You can also serve this on any type of bread you like. Ciabatta or focaccia would be delicious.*

Mushroom *and* Provolone Patty Melts

HANDS-ON TIME: 27 min. **TOTAL TIME:** 35 min.

PREP TIP *This filling sandwich mimics the heftier diner staple perfectly, only with significantly fewer calories. Serve with roasted potato wedges, which can bake while you make the sandwiches.*

- 1 tablespoon olive oil
- ¼ cup thinly sliced yellow onion
- ⅛ teaspoon salt
- ⅛ teaspoon freshly ground black pepper
- 1 (8-ounce) package sliced cremini mushrooms
- 1½ teaspoons all-purpose flour
- ¼ cup dark beer (such as porter)
- 1 pound ground sirloin
- Cooking spray
- 8 (1.1-ounce) slices rye bread
- 4 (¾-ounce) slices reduced-fat provolone cheese

Heat a skillet over medium-high heat. Add oil to pan; swirl to coat. Add onion, salt, pepper, and mushrooms; sauté 3 minutes. Sprinkle flour over mushroom mixture; cook 1 minute, stirring constantly. Stir in beer; cook 30 seconds or until thick. Remove from heat; keep warm.

Heat a large skillet over medium-high heat. Shape beef into 4 (4-inch) patties. Coat pan with cooking spray. Add patties; cook 4 minutes on each side or until done; remove from pan.

Wipe pan clean; heat over medium-high heat. Coat 1 side of each bread slice with cooking spray. Place 4 bread slices, coated sides down, in pan. Top each with 1 patty, 1 cheese slice, and one-fourth of mushroom mixture. Top with remaining bread slices; coat with cooking spray. Cook 2 minutes on each side or until browned. Serves 4 (serving size: 1 sandwich)

Calories 416; Fat 17.1g (sat 6.2g, mono 7.7g, poly 1.4g); Protein 30g; Carb 34.3g; Fiber 4.1g; Chol 42mg; Iron 3.9mg; Sodium 708mg; Calc 232mg

Italian Meatball Sliders

HANDS-ON TIME: 26 min. **TOTAL TIME:** 34 min.

 PREP TIP *Adding ricotta to meatballs keeps them moist. You can make the meatballs ahead and freeze them for a quick meal on busy nights. Serve with a spinach salad, which you can prep while the meatballs simmer.*

1 tablespoon olive oil, divided
3 garlic cloves, minced
3 shallots, finely diced
⅓ cup part-skim ricotta cheese
¼ cup chopped fresh parsley
¼ cup panko (Japanese breadcrumbs), toasted
½ teaspoon black pepper
¼ teaspoon crushed red pepper

⅛ teaspoon salt
8 ounces lean ground pork
2 (4-ounce) links turkey Italian sausage, casings removed
1 large egg
1½ cups lower-sodium marinara sauce
12 slider buns, toasted
12 large basil leaves

1 **Heat a large skillet** over medium heat. Add 1 teaspoon oil to pan; swirl to coat. Add garlic and shallots; sauté 3 minutes or until shallots are softened.

2 **Combine shallot mixture,** ricotta, and next 8 ingredients (through egg) in a medium bowl. Shape mixture into 12 (1-inch) meatballs; flatten each meatball slightly.

3 **Return pan** to medium-high heat. Add 2 teaspoons oil to pan; swirl to coat. Add meatballs; cook 6 minutes. Add marinara sauce; bring to a boil, scraping pan to loosen browned bits. Cover, reduce heat, and simmer 8 minutes or until meatballs are done. Top bottom half of each bun with 1½ tablespoons sauce, 1 meatball, 1 basil leaf, and top half of bun. Serves 6 (serving size: 2 sliders)

Calories 429; Fat 16.3g (sat 4g, mono 5.1g, poly 4.2g); Protein 25.4g; Carb 60.5g; Fiber 2.3g; Chol 85mg; Iron 2.7mg; Sodium 764mg; Calc 131mg

 SIMPLE SWAP *Substitute regular dry breadcrumbs for panko. To toast, pour them into a small skillet over medium heat. Cook 5 minutes or until golden brown, shaking pan often.*

Pulled Chicken Sandwiches *with* Mango Slaw

HANDS-ON TIME: 25 min. **TOTAL TIME:** 35 min.

 PREP TIP *Prep the ingredients for the mango slaw while the chicken simmers for an easy, fresh, toss-together side dish.*

3 tablespoons ketchup
1 tablespoon cider vinegar
1 tablespoon prepared mustard
1 tablespoon molasses
¾ teaspoon chili powder
½ teaspoon ground cumin
¼ teaspoon freshly ground black pepper
⅛ teaspoon ground ginger
12 ounces skinless, boneless chicken thighs, cut into 2-inch pieces

4 cups packaged cabbage-and-carrot coleslaw
1 cup chopped peeled mango
¼ cup vertically sliced red onion
¼ cup canola mayonnaise
1 tablespoon sugar
1 tablespoon cider vinegar
¼ teaspoon salt
4 (2-ounce) sandwich rolls, cut in half horizontally
12 dill pickle chips

1 **Combine first 9 ingredients** in a medium saucepan; bring to a boil. Reduce heat to medium-low; cover and cook, stirring occasionally, 25 minutes or until chicken is done and tender. Remove from heat; shred with 2 forks to measure 2 cups meat.

 2 **While chicken simmers, combine coleslaw,** mango, and onion in a large bowl. Add mayonnaise, sugar, cider vinegar, and salt; toss well to coat.

 3 **Place ½ cup chicken** on bottom half of each roll. Top each with 3 pickles and top half of roll. Serve slaw with sandwiches. Serves 4 (serving size: 1 sandwich and about 1 cup slaw)

Calories 306; Fat 12.3g (sat 1.9g, mono 5.8g, poly 3.3g); Protein 14g; Carb 33.8g; Fiber 2.5g; Chol 56mg; Iron 2.1mg; Sodium 512mg; Calc 103mg

SIMPLE SWAP *You can make this with any type of meat you might have, like sliced pork chops, pork tenderloin, or grilled steak. Use Monterey Jack with jalapeños for a little more chile pepper punch.*

184

Chicken *and* Black Bean– Stuffed Burritos

HANDS-ON TIME: 25 min. **TOTAL TIME:** 25 min.

 These skillet-grilled burritos come together in a flash thanks to rotisserie chicken. Keep this meal light by serving it with a salad topped with sliced avocado and fresh radish.

- ¼ cup water
- 2 tablespoons fresh lime juice
- ½ teaspoon chili powder
- ¼ teaspoon ground cumin
- ¼ teaspoon freshly ground black pepper
- ⅛ teaspoon ground red pepper
- 2 cups shredded skinless, boneless rotisserie chicken breast
- ¼ cup thinly sliced green onions
- ¾ cup cooked black beans
- ½ cup refrigerated fresh salsa
- 4 (8-inch) flour tortillas
- 2 ounces shredded Monterey Jack cheese (about ½ cup)
- Cooking spray

 Bring first 6 ingredients to a boil in a small saucepan. Stir in chicken and onions.

 Combine beans and salsa in a small bowl. Spoon ¼ cup bean mixture and ½ cup chicken mixture down center of each tortilla; sprinkle with 2 tablespoons cheese. Roll up.

 Heat a large skillet over medium-high heat. Coat pan with cooking spray. Add 2 burritos. Place a cast-iron or other heavy skillet on top of burritos, and cook 3 minutes on each side. Remove from pan, and repeat procedure with remaining burritos. Serves 4 (serving size: 1 burrito)

Calories 353; Fat 9.8g (sat 4.1g, mono 3.6g, poly 1.3g); Protein 30.9g; Carb 33.1g; Fiber 2.4g; Chol 72mg; Iron 1.6mg; Sodium 595mg; Calc 137mg

Spicy Chicken Quesadillas

HANDS-ON TIME: 16 min. **TOTAL TIME:** 16 min.

 PREP TIP *To make these quesadillas kid-friendly, omit the pickled jalapeño peppers.*

SIMPLE SWAP *Use any type of beans you like, and add fresh baby spinach for a dose of green.*

- 1 cup chopped skinless, boneless rotisserie chicken breast
- 1/3 cup refrigerated fresh salsa
- 1/4 cup canned unsalted black beans, rinsed and drained
- 1/4 cup frozen whole-kernel corn, thawed
- 1½ tablespoons chopped pickled jalapeño pepper
- 8 (6-inch) flour tortillas
- 4 ounces shredded reduced-fat Monterey Jack cheese (about 1 cup)
- Cooking spray
- 1/4 cup reduced-fat sour cream

 1 Combine first 5 ingredients in a medium bowl.

 2 Divide chicken mixture evenly over 4 tortillas. Sprinkle quesadillas evenly with cheese. Top with remaining tortillas.

3 Heat a large skillet over medium-high heat. Coat pan with cooking spray. Add 1 quesadilla to pan; cook 1 minute on each side or until golden. Remove from pan, and repeat with remaining quesadillas. Serve with sour cream. Serves 4 (serving size: 1 quesadilla and 1 tablespoon sour cream)

Calories 372; Fat 14.1g (sat 6.2g, mono 5g, poly 1.3g); Protein 24.2g; Carb 36.7g; Fiber 2.7g; Chol 56mg; Iron 2.6mg; Sodium 743mg; Calc 307mg

Chicken *and* Waffle Sandwiches

HANDS-ON TIME: 7 min. **TOTAL TIME:** 15 min.

 PREP TIP *The full-flavored sauce pairs nicely with the chicken and bacon. Toast the waffles while the bacon cooks.*

- 4 **lower-sodium bacon slices, halved crosswise**
- 3 **tablespoons canola mayonnaise**
- 1 **tablespoon low-fat buttermilk**
- 1 **teaspoon cider vinegar**
- ¼ **teaspoon sugar**
- ¼ **teaspoon garlic powder**
- ⅛ **teaspoon freshly ground black pepper**
- 8 **frozen whole-grain waffles, toasted**
- 6 **ounces thinly sliced lower-sodium deli chicken breast**
- 8 **(¼-inch-thick) slices ripe tomato**
- 4 **Boston lettuce leaves**

 1 **Cook bacon** in a large nonstick skillet over medium heat until crisp. Drain on paper towels.

 2 **Combine mayonnaise** and next 5 ingredients (through pepper) in a small bowl.

3 **Spread mayonnaise mixture** evenly over 4 waffles. Divide chicken, bacon, tomato, and lettuce evenly among servings. Top with remaining waffles. Serves 4 (serving size: 1 sandwich)

 SIMPLE SWAP *Use whatever lettuce you have on hand or sub smoked turkey for the chicken breast.*

Calories 355; Fat 19.5g (sat 2g, mono 7.6g, poly 7.4g); Protein 16.3g; Carb 33.5g; Fiber 6.6g; Chol 39mg; Iron 2mg; Sodium 739mg; Calc 32mg

Substitute hot
Italian sausage—
for a spicier kick—
or whatever type
you have on hand.

Italian Sausage Hoagies

HANDS-ON TIME: 14 min. **TOTAL TIME:** 20 min.

 PREP TIP *Prechopped onion helps get these hearty sandwiches on the table fast. Garnish with fresh basil leaves, if you like.*

- 4 (2-ounce) hoagie rolls, halved lengthwise
- 9 ounces sweet turkey Italian sausage, cut into 1-inch-thick pieces
- ½ cup prechopped onion
- 1 teaspoon minced fresh garlic

- 1 cup lower-sodium marinara sauce
- 1 small red bell pepper, thinly sliced
- ¼ teaspoon freshly ground black pepper
- 2.25 ounces shredded part-skim mozzarella cheese (about ½ cup)

1 **Preheat broiler.** Hollow out top halves of rolls. Arrange rolls, cut sides up, on a baking sheet. Broil 1½ minutes or until toasted. Set aside.

2 **Heat a large skillet** over medium-high heat. Add sausage to pan; cook 2 minutes or until lightly browned, stirring occasionally. Add onion and garlic; cook 1 minute. Add marinara, bell pepper, and black pepper; bring to a boil. Reduce heat, and simmer 6 minutes or until bell pepper is crisp-tender.

3 **Arrange about ¾ cup** sausage mixture over bottom half of each roll; sprinkle each serving with about 2 tablespoons cheese. Place on a baking sheet; broil 2 minutes or until cheese melts. Top with top halves of rolls. Serves 4 (serving size: 1 hoagie)

Calories 309; Fat 7g (sat 4.4g, mono 0.9g, poly 0.1g); Protein 20.7g; Carb 28.5g; Fiber 2.5g; Chol 51mg; Iron 1.8mg; Sodium 588mg; Calc 182mg

6

1-step sides »

These simple salads, vegetables, and grain side dishes offer delicious ways to easily round out a meal.

Frisée *and* Arugula Salad

HANDS-ON TIME: 12 min. **TOTAL TIME:** 12 min.

- - - - - - - - - -

¼ cup canola mayonnaise
1 tablespoon chopped fresh dill
2 tablespoons water
1 tablespoon sherry vinegar
1½ teaspoons Dijon mustard
½ teaspoon freshly ground black pepper
⅛ teaspoon salt

2 cups frisée
2 cups baby arugula
½ cup thinly sliced fennel bulb
½ cup thinly sliced cucumber
½ cup thinly sliced radish
2 tablespoons toasted pine nuts

1. Combine first 7 ingredients in a large bowl; stir with a whisk. Add frisée and next 4 ingredients (through radish); toss gently to combine. Sprinkle with toasted pine nuts. Serves 4

Calories 147; Fat 14.1g (sat 0.7g, mono 4.3g, poly 8.5g); Protein 1.5g; Carb 4.1g; Fiber 1.8g; Chol 5mg; Iron 0.8mg; Sodium 229mg; Calc 42mg

Romaine Salad *with* Balsamic Vinaigrette »

HANDS-ON TIME: 11 min. **TOTAL TIME:** 11 min.

- - - - - - - - - -

 PREP TIP *To save even more time, you can start with precut romaine.*

3 tablespoons balsamic vinegar
2 tablespoons olive oil
1 tablespoon minced shallots
1 tablespoon chopped fresh parsley

1 teaspoon Dijon mustard
¼ teaspoon freshly ground black pepper
⅛ teaspoon salt
1 garlic clove, crushed
6 cups chopped romaine lettuce
¼ cup dried cherries, chopped
2 tablespoons crumbled feta cheese

1. Combine first 8 ingredients in a large bowl; stir well with a whisk. Add lettuce, dried cherries, and cheese; toss gently to coat. Serves 4 (serving size: 1½ cups)

Calories 131; Fat 8g (sat 1.7g, mono 5.2g, poly 0.9g); Protein 2g; Carb 13.1g; Fiber 2.6g; Chol 4mg; Iron 1.2mg; Sodium 167mg; Calc 64mg

SIMPLE SWAP *Customize this basic salad by using other fruit, such as dried cranberries, apricots, or raisins, or different cheeses, like blue or goat cheese.*

SIMPLE
SWAP

Make with
baby arugula
or mixed
greens instead
of spinach.

Spinach Salad
« *with* Garlic Vinaigrette

HANDS-ON TIME: 6 min. **TOTAL TIME:** 6 min.

- - - - - - - - - -

 Baby spinach helps streamline prep since you won't spend time removing the stems.

1½ tablespoons extra-virgin olive oil
1 tablespoon white wine vinegar
½ teaspoon Dijon mustard
¼ teaspoon freshly ground black pepper
⅛ teaspoon salt
2 garlic cloves, minced
6 cups fresh baby spinach (about 6 ounces)
¼ cup vertically sliced red onion

1. Combine first 6 ingredients in a large bowl, stirring well with a whisk. Add spinach and onion; toss to coat. Serves 4 (serving size: 1¾ cups)

Calories 66; Fat 5.1g (sat 0.7g, mono 3.7g, poly 0.5g); Protein 1.1g; Carb 5.2g; Fiber 1.9g; Chol 0mg; Iron 1.3mg; Sodium 147mg; Calc 31mg

Napa Cabbage Slaw

HANDS-ON TIME: 15 min. **TOTAL TIME:** 25 min.

- - - - - - - - - -

 Thinly slicing the vegetables is key to the texture of this slaw.

1 tablespoon lower-sodium soy sauce
1 tablespoon dark sesame oil
1 tablespoon rice vinegar
1½ teaspoons sweet chili sauce
1 teaspoon grated peeled fresh ginger
¼ teaspoon crushed red pepper
2 cups thinly sliced napa (Chinese) cabbage
½ cup julienne-cut yellow squash
½ cup matchstick-cut carrot
¼ cup diagonally cut green onions

1. Combine first 6 ingredients in a large bowl. Add remaining ingredients; toss well. Let stand 10 minutes. Serves 4 (serving size: ¾ cup)

Calories 52; Fat 3.5g (sat 0.5g, mono 1.4g, poly 1.5g); Protein 1.1g; Carb 4.4g; Fiber 1.4g; Chol 0mg; Iron 0.2mg; Sodium 117mg; Calc 43mg

SIMPLE SWAP *Top with feta or fresh mozzarella instead of goat cheese.*

Garlicky Asparagus

HANDS-ON TIME: 7 min. **TOTAL TIME:** 15 min.

- - - - - - - - -

Sauté the thinly sliced garlic while the asparagus steams.

- **1 pound asparagus spears, trimmed**
- **1 tablespoon olive oil**
- **2 garlic cloves, thinly sliced**
- **1/8 teaspoon salt**
- **1/8 teaspoon freshly ground black pepper**

1. Steam asparagus 4 minutes or until crisp-tender. Heat a large skillet over medium heat. Add oil to pan; swirl to coat. Add garlic; cook 2 minutes or until fragrant, stirring frequently. Add asparagus, salt, and pepper; toss to combine. Serves 4

Calories 57; Fat 3.4g (sat 0.5g, mono 2.5g, poly 0.4g); Protein 2.5g; Carb 5.4g; Fiber 2.5g; Chol 0mg; Iron 0.5mg; Sodium 74mg; Calc 27mg

You can prepare this using 2 (8-ounce) packages of microwave-in-a-bag asparagus spears, if you like, or substitute trimmed green beans.

Asparagus *with* « Balsamic Tomatoes

HANDS-ON TIME: 18 min. **TOTAL TIME:** 18 min.

- - - - - - - - -

Begin cooking the tomatoes and garlic while the asparagus cooks.

- **1 pound asparagus spears, trimmed**
- **2 teaspoons extra-virgin olive oil**
- **1 1/2 cups halved grape tomatoes**

- **1/2 teaspoon minced fresh garlic**
- **2 tablespoons balsamic vinegar**
- **1/4 teaspoon salt**
- **3 tablespoons crumbled goat cheese**
- **1/2 teaspoon freshly ground black pepper**

1. Cook asparagus in boiling water 2 minutes or until crisp-tender. Drain. Heat a large skillet over medium-high heat. Add oil to pan; swirl to coat. Add tomatoes and garlic; cook 5 minutes. Stir in vinegar; cook 3 minutes. Stir in salt. Arrange asparagus on a platter; top with tomato mixture. Sprinkle with cheese and pepper. Serves 4

Calories 69; Fat 3.9g (sat 1.4g, mono 2g, poly 0.3g); Protein 3g; Carb 6.5g; Fiber 2.1g; Chol 4mg; Iron 1.6mg; Sodium 181mg; Calc 45mg

Lemony Bean Salad »

HANDS-ON TIME: 7 min. **TOTAL TIME:** 7 min.

- - - - - - - - - -

PREP TIP *Use a vegetable peeler to easily shave the Parmigiano-Reggiano.*

2 tablespoons fresh lemon juice
2 teaspoons extra-virgin olive oil
½ teaspoon minced fresh garlic
¼ teaspoon Dijon mustard

⅛ teaspoon freshly ground black pepper
⅛ teaspoon sugar
¼ cup finely chopped red onion
2 tablespoons chopped fresh parsley
1 (15-ounce) can cannellini beans or other white beans, rinsed and drained
2 tablespoons shaved fresh Parmigiano-Reggiano cheese

1. Combine first 6 ingredients in a large bowl, stirring with a whisk. Add onion, parsley, and beans; toss gently to coat. Top with Parmigiano-Reggiano. Serves 4 (serving size: ½ cup)

Calories 100; Fat 3.1g (sat 0.8g, mono 2g, poly 0.3g); Protein 5.6g; Carb 13g; Fiber 3.6g; Chol 2mg; Iron 1.2mg; Sodium 159mg; Calc 67mg

Beets *with* Shallot Vinaigrette »

HANDS-ON TIME: 12 min. **TOTAL TIME:** 20 min.

- - - - - - - - - -

PREP TIP *Slice the shallots and combine the rest of the ingredients while the beets cook.*

1½ pounds halved peeled beets
2 tablespoons sliced shallots

1½ tablespoons red wine vinegar
1 tablespoon extra-virgin olive oil
½ teaspoon Dijon mustard
¼ teaspoon freshly ground black pepper
⅛ teaspoon salt

1. Wrap beets in parchment paper. Microwave at HIGH until tender (about 7 minutes). Let stand 5 minutes. Cut into 1-inch pieces. Combine shallots and remaining ingredients in a medium bowl; stir well with a whisk. Add beets; toss gently to coat. Serves 4 (serving size: about ⅔ cup)

Calories 110; Fat 3.7g (sat 0.5g, mono 2.5g, poly 0.5g); Protein 2.9g; Carb 17.6g; Fiber 5g; Chol 0mg; Iron 1.5mg; Sodium 253mg; Calc 30mg

SIMPLE SWAP

Make with chickpeas (garbanzo beans) instead of cannellini.

SIMPLE SWAP

You can use red or golden beets—or a mix.

Roasted Brussels Sprouts *with* Hazelnuts

HANDS-ON TIME: 8 min. **TOTAL TIME:** 25 min.

- - - - - - - - - -

¼ cup chopped hazelnuts
2 teaspoons canola oil
1½ teaspoons maple syrup
½ teaspoon freshly ground black pepper
¼ teaspoon salt
1 pound halved trimmed Brussels sprouts

1. Preheat oven to 425°.
Combine all ingredients on a jelly-roll pan; toss to coat. Bake at 425° for 17 minutes, stirring once. Serves 4 (serving size: about ½ cup)

Calories 117; Fat 7g (sat 0.6g, mono 4.8g, poly 1.4g); Protein 4.6g; Carb 12.2g; Fiber 4.7g; Chol 0mg; Iron 1.8mg; Sodium 173mg; Calc 55mg

 SIMPLE SWAP *Make with trimmed asparagus spears, green beans, or broccoli florets instead of Brussels sprouts. You can substitute pecans or walnuts for the hazelnuts.*

Spicy Chile *and* « Garlic Broccoli

HANDS-ON TIME: 14 min. **TOTAL TIME:** 20 min.

- - - - - - - - - -

PREP TIP *Instead of steaming broccoli, use a 12-ounce package of microwave-in-a-bag broccoli.*

12 ounces broccoli florets (5 cups)
2 tablespoons extra-virgin olive oil
1½ teaspoons crushed red pepper
4 garlic cloves, sliced
1 tablespoon fresh lemon juice
1 teaspoon grated lemon rind
¼ teaspoon kosher salt

1. Arrange broccoli in a steamer. Steam, covered, 4 minutes or until crisp-tender. Place broccoli in a large bowl. Heat a small skillet over medium-high heat. Add oil to pan; swirl to coat. Add pepper and garlic; cook 2 minutes. Add juice. Pour oil mixture over broccoli. Sprinkle with rind and salt. Serves 6 (serving size: ⅔ cup)

Calories 61; Fat 4.8g (sat 0.7g, mono 3.3g, poly 0.6g); Protein 1.9g; Carb 4.1g; Fiber 1.9g; Chol 0mg; Iron 0.6mg; Sodium 96mg; Calc 32mg

Lemon-Parmesan Broccoli ›»

HANDS-ON TIME: 14 min. **TOTAL TIME:** 20 min.

- - - - - - - - - -

 Mince and sauté the garlic while the broccoli steams.

- **12** ounces broccoli florets (5 cups)
- **2** tablespoons extra-virgin olive oil
- **2** garlic cloves, minced
- **½** teaspoon grated lemon rind
- **1** teaspoon fresh lemon juice
- **¼** teaspoon kosher salt
- **3** tablespoons shaved fresh Parmesan cheese

1. Arrange broccoli in a steamer. Steam, covered, 4 minutes or until crisp-tender. Place broccoli in a large bowl. Heat a small skillet over medium-high heat. Add oil to pan; swirl to coat. Add garlic; cook 2 minutes or until fragrant. Add oil mixture, rind, juice, and salt to broccoli; toss to coat. Sprinkle broccoli mixture with cheese. Serves 6 (serving size: ⅔ cup)

Calories 71; Fat 5.7g (sat 1.2g, mono 3.3g, poly 0.6g); Protein 2.9g; Carb 3.5g; Fiber 1.7g; Chol 3mg; Iron 0.5mg; Sodium 146mg; Calc 67mg

 You can also prepare this side with thinly sliced summer squash and zucchini.

Butter-Roasted Carrots

HANDS-ON TIME: 5 min. **TOTAL TIME:** 20 min.

- - - - - - - - - -

- **2** cups (2-inch) diagonally cut carrot
- **1** tablespoon butter, melted
- **1** teaspoon olive oil
- **¼** teaspoon kosher salt
- **¼** teaspoon freshly ground black pepper
- Cooking spray

1. Preheat oven to 425°.
Combine first 5 ingredients on a baking sheet coated with cooking spray; toss to coat. Bake at 425° for 15 minutes. Serves 4 (serving size: about ½ cup)

Calories 61; Fat 4.2g (sat 2g, mono 1.6g, poly 0.3g); Protein 0.6g; Carb 5.9g; Fiber 1.7g; Chol 8mg; Iron 0.2mg; Sodium 183mg; Calc 22mg

 This simple preparation works with virtually any vegetable. Try it with thinly sliced Brussels sprouts or parsnips.

SIMPLE SWAP

Use chopped walnuts or pecans instead of pine nuts.

Citus Green
« Beans *with* Pine Nuts

HANDS-ON TIME: 15 min. **TOTAL TIME:** 22 min.

- - - - - - - - - -

PREP TIP *You can toast the pine nuts in a small dry skillet. Watch them carefully and shake the pan frequently—they can go from toasty to burned in seconds.*

- 1 pound green beans, trimmed
- 2 teaspoons extra-virgin olive oil

- ¾ cup sliced shallots (about 2 large)
- 1 teaspoon grated orange rind
- 1 tablespoon fresh orange juice
- ¼ teaspoon freshly ground black pepper
- ⅛ teaspoon coarse sea salt
- 1 tablespoon pine nuts, toasted

1. Cook green beans in boiling water 2 minutes. Drain and rinse under cold running water. Drain well. Heat a large nonstick skillet over medium-high heat. Add oil to pan; swirl to coat. Add shallots; sauté 2 minutes or until tender. Add green beans; stir well. Add rind, juice, pepper, and salt; sauté 2 minutes. Spoon onto a platter; sprinkle with nuts. Serves 4 (serving size: 1 cup)

Calories 86; Fat 3.8g (sat 0.4g, mono 2.1g, poly 1.1g); Protein 2.5g; Carb 12.8g; Fiber 4.5g; Chol 0mg; Iron 1mg; Sodium 76mg; Calc 68mg

Garlic-Basil Corn

HANDS-ON TIME: 7 min. **TOTAL TIME:** 11 min.

- - - - - - - - - -

- 1 tablespoon butter, softened
- 1 tablespoon chopped fresh basil
- 1 garlic clove, minced
- 4 ears shucked corn

1. Combine first 3 ingredients in a small bowl. Place corn in a large saucepan of boiling water; cook 4 minutes. Drain. Spoon 1 teaspoon butter mixture over each ear of corn. Serves 4 (serving size: 1 ear)

Calories 114; Fat 4.3g (sat 2.2g, mono 1.2g, poly 0.6g); Protein 3.4g; Carb 19.3g; Fiber 2.1g; Chol 8mg; Iron 0.6mg; Sodium 41mg; Calc 5mg

SIMPLE SWAP

Make with snow peas instead of sugar snap peas.

206

Stewed Okra *and* Fresh Tomato

HANDS-ON TIME: 6 min. **TOTAL TIME:** 28 min.

- - - - - - - - - -

2 teaspoons olive oil
¾ cup chopped onion
1 pound fresh okra pods
1 cup chopped tomato
1 cup organic vegetable broth
¾ cup fresh corn kernels
⅛ teaspoon salt

1. Heat a Dutch oven over medium-high heat. Add oil to pan; swirl to coat. Add onion; sauté 2 minutes. Add okra and remaining ingredients to pan; bring to a boil. Cover, reduce heat, and simmer 20 minutes or until vegetables are tender, stirring occasionally. Serves 4 (serving size: about 1¼ cups)

Calories 97; Fat 2.8g (sat 0.5g, mono 1.8g, poly 0.4g); Protein 3.6g; Carb 17.2g; Fiber 4.7g; Chol 0mg; Iron 1.1mg; Sodium 227mg; Calc 91mg

« Lemony Snap Peas

HANDS-ON TIME: 6 min. **TOTAL TIME:** 6 min.

- - - - - - - - - -

PREP TIP *To save time, look for already trimmed sugar snap peas in the produce section. Put the water on to boil while you prep your ingredients.*

12 ounces sugar snap peas, trimmed
½ teaspoon grated lemon rind
2 tablespoons fresh lemon juice

1 tablespoon extra-virgin olive oil
1 teaspoon Dijon mustard
½ teaspoon sugar
¼ teaspoon kosher salt
¼ teaspoon freshly ground black pepper
1 shallot, minced

1. Cook peas in boiling water 30 seconds or until crisp-tender. Drain and plunge into ice water; drain. Slice half of peas diagonally. Combine rind and remaining ingredients in a medium bowl; stir with a whisk. Add peas; toss to coat. Serves 4 (serving size: about 1 cup)

Calories 73; Fat 3.6g (sat 0.5g, mono 2.5g, poly 0.4g); Protein 2.5g; Carb 8.4g; Fiber 2.3g; Chol 0mg; Iron 1.8mg; Sodium 154mg; Calc 39mg

Roasted Potatoes
and Haricots Verts ››

HANDS-ON TIME: 5 min. **TOTAL TIME:** 30 min.

- - - - - - - - - -

 PREP TIP *Small fingerlings become deliciously fluffy inside when they're roasted. Red-fleshed fingerling potatoes are waxier than yellow-fleshed, so they crisp on the outside; use whatever variety you can find, though, since either will work.*

1 tablespoon olive oil
¼ teaspoon salt
¼ teaspoon freshly ground
  black pepper
1 pound fingerling potatoes,
  halved lengthwise
10 ounces trimmed haricots verts
  (French green beans)
2 garlic cloves, thinly sliced
Cooking spray

1. Preheat oven to 425°. Combine first 6 ingredients on a jelly-roll pan coated with cooking spray; toss to coat. Bake at 425° on bottom rack 25 minutes, stirring once. Serves 4 (serving size: 1 cup)

Calories 145; Fat 3.8g (sat 0.5g, mono 2.5g, poly 0.5g); Protein 3.8g; Carb 26g; Fiber 3.5g; Chol 0mg; Iron 1.8mg; Sodium 158mg; Calc 44mg

Garlic Mashed Potatoes

HANDS-ON TIME: 10 min. **TOTAL TIME:** 30 min.

- - - - - - - - - -

 PREP TIP *Leave the skins on the potatoes for added texture and color and quicker prep.*

2 pounds cubed peeled red potatoes
2 garlic cloves, halved

½ cup 2% reduced-fat milk
1 tablespoon butter
¼ teaspoon salt
¼ teaspoon freshly ground
  black pepper

1. Place potatoes and garlic in a medium saucepan; cover with cold water. Bring to a boil. Reduce heat, and simmer 12 minutes or until potatoes are very tender. Drain. Return potato mixture to pan. Add milk, butter, salt, and pepper; mash with a potato masher to desired consistency. Serves 4 (serving size: about 1 cup)

Calories 202; Fat 3.8g (sat 2.3g, mono 0.9g, poly 0.3g); Protein 5.4g; Carb 38.1g; Fiber 3.9g; Chol 10mg; Iron 1.7mg; Sodium 194mg; Calc 63mg

SIMPLE SWAP ***If you can't find fingerlings, use red potatoes cut into 1-inch pieces. Substitute green beans for the haricots verts.***

Spicy Sweet Potato Wedges

HANDS-ON TIME: 5 min. **TOTAL TIME:** 25 min.

- - - - - - - - - -

PREP TIP *Cooking these sweet potato wedges at a high heat makes their interior tender and caramelizes the sugar-and-spice coating, browning the outside. This recipe can be cut in half.*

- **6 medium sweet potatoes (about 2¼ pounds)**
- **Cooking spray**
- **2 teaspoons sugar**
- **½ teaspoon salt**
- **¼ teaspoon ground red pepper**
- **⅛ teaspoon freshly ground black pepper**

1. Preheat oven to 500°.

While oven preheats, peel potatoes; cut each lengthwise into quarters. Place potatoes in a large bowl; coat with cooking spray. Combine sugar, salt, and peppers, and sprinkle over potatoes, tossing well to coat. Arrange potatoes, cut sides down, in a single layer on a baking sheet. Bake at 500° for 10 minutes; turn wedges over. Bake an additional 10 minutes or until tender and beginning to brown. Serves 8 (serving size: 3 wedges)

Calories 153; Fat 0.4g (sat 0.1g, mono 0g, poly 0.2g); Protein 2.4g; Carb 35.5g; Fiber 2.3g; Chol 0mg; Iron 0.9mg; Sodium 166mg; Calc 31mg

Herbed Couscous Pilaf ››

HANDS-ON TIME: 15 min. **TOTAL TIME:** 15 min.

- - - - - - - - - -

- **1 tablespoon olive oil**
- **¼ cup finely chopped shallots**
- **1 cup uncooked couscous**
- **1 cup plus 2 tablespoons fat-free, lower-sodium chicken broth**
- **⅛ teaspoon salt**
- **1 tablespoon chopped fresh flat-leaf parsley**
- **1 teaspoon chopped fresh thyme**

1. Heat a small saucepan over medium-high heat. Add oil to pan; swirl to coat. Add shallots, and sauté 2 minutes or until tender. Stir in couscous; sauté 1 minute. Add broth and salt; bring to a boil. Cover, remove from heat, and let stand 5 minutes. Fluff with a fork. Stir in parsley and thyme. Serves 4 (serving size: ¾ cup)

Calories 205; Fat 3.7g (sat 0.5g, mono 2.5g, poly 0.5g); Protein 6.5g; Carb 35.6g; Fiber 2.6g; Chol 0mg; Iron 0.8mg; Sodium 189mg; Calc 20mg

SIMPLE SWAP *To make this side vegetarian, use vegetable broth instead of chicken broth.*

SIMPLE SWAP

You can also prepare this side with fresh yellow summer squash.

Roasted Summer Squash *with* Parsley

HANDS-ON TIME: 7 min. **TOTAL TIME:** 24 min.

- - - - - - - - - -

 Chop the zucchini and yellow squash while the oven preheats.

2 cups chopped zucchini
2 cups chopped yellow squash

¼ teaspoon salt
¼ teaspoon freshly ground black pepper
¼ cup chopped fresh parsley

1. Preheat oven to 425°. Arrange zucchini and yellow squash in a single layer on a jelly-roll pan; sprinkle with salt and pepper. Bake at 425° for 17 minutes or until crisp-tender. Toss with parsley. Serves 4 (serving size: about ½ cup)

Calories 24; Fat 0.4g (sat 0.1g, mono 0.1g, poly 0.1g); Protein 1.5g; Carb 4.6g; Fiber 1.2g; Chol 0mg; Iron 0.7mg; Sodium 155mg; Calc 28mg

---

« Zucchini Oven Chips

HANDS-ON TIME: 10 min. **TOTAL TIME:** 40 min.

- - - - - - - - - -

 Breaded, baked, amazingly crispy zucchini chips taste like they're fried. They are a healthy substitute for French fries or potato chips.

¼ cup dry breadcrumbs
1 ounce grated fresh Parmesan cheese (about ¼ cup)

¼ teaspoon seasoned salt
¼ teaspoon garlic powder
⅛ teaspoon freshly ground black pepper
2 tablespoons fat-free milk
2½ cups (¼-inch-thick) slices zucchini (about 2 small)
Cooking spray

1. Preheat oven to 425°. Combine first 5 ingredients in a medium bowl, stirring with a whisk. Place milk in a shallow bowl. Dip zucchini slices in milk, and dredge in breadcrumb mixture. Place coated slices on an ovenproof wire rack coated with cooking spray; place rack on a baking sheet. Bake at 425° for 30 minutes or until browned and crisp. Serve immediately. Serves 4 (serving size: about ¾ cup)

Calories 61; Fat 1.9g (sat 1g, mono 0.5g, poly 0.2g); Protein 3.8g; Carb 7.6g; Fiber 1g; Chol 5mg; Iron 0.6mg; Sodium 231mg; Calc 87mg

Creamed Spinach *and* Mushrooms ››

HANDS-ON TIME: 19 min. **TOTAL TIME:** 19 min.

- - - - - - - - - -

 Try this fresh take on a steakhouse favorite. Don't skip the nutmeg—it brightens the flavor of this side dish.

4 teaspoons canola oil, divided
8 ounces sliced cremini mushrooms
1 (10-ounce) package fresh baby spinach
1/3 cup finely chopped shallots

2 teaspoons minced fresh garlic
3/4 cup fat-free milk
1 tablespoon all-purpose flour
3/8 teaspoon salt
1/4 teaspoon freshly ground black pepper
Dash of nutmeg
2 1/2 ounces 1/3-less-fat cream cheese

1. Heat a large skillet over medium-high heat. Add 1½ teaspoons oil to pan; swirl to coat. Add mushrooms; cook 6 minutes or until liquid evaporates. Remove mushrooms from pan. Add 1½ teaspoons oil to pan; swirl to coat. Add spinach; cook 1 minute or until spinach wilts. Remove from heat. Heat a Dutch oven over medium heat. Add 1 teaspoon oil to pan; swirl to coat. Add shallots and garlic; cook 1 minute, stirring constantly. Combine milk and flour, stirring with a whisk. Add milk mixture, salt, pepper, and nutmeg to pan; bring to a boil, stirring constantly. Cook 3 minutes or until thickened, stirring constantly. Add cheese; stir until cheese melts and mixture is smooth. Add mushrooms and spinach to milk mixture, and toss gently to coat. Serves 6 (serving size: ½ cup)

Calories 102; Fat 6.1g (sat 1.8g, mono 2.7g, poly 1.1g); Protein 4.8g; Carb 8.1g; Fiber 1.4g; Chol 9mg; Iron 1.7mg; Sodium 241mg; Calc 111mg

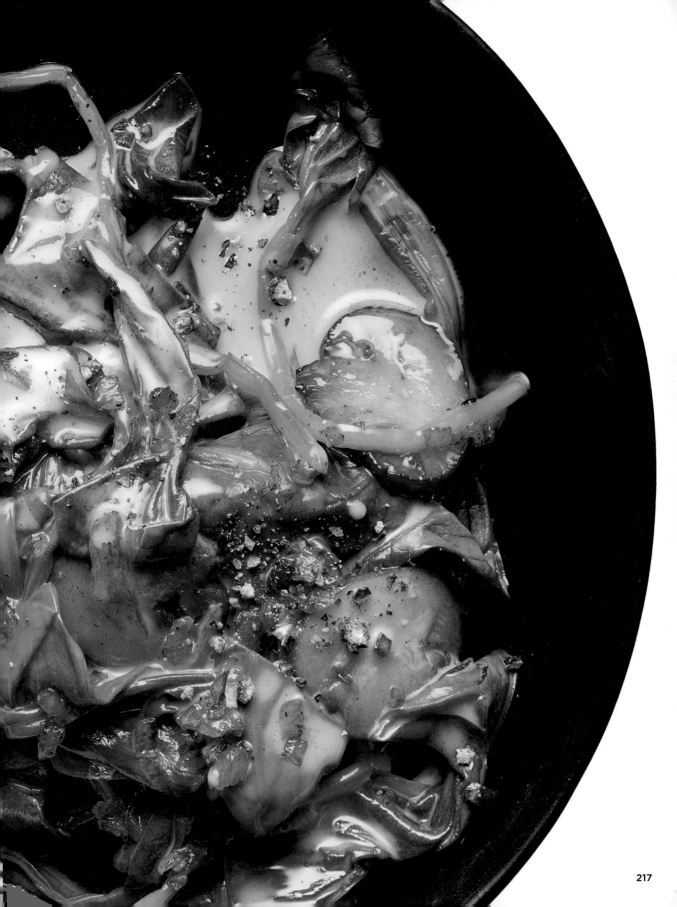

Nutritional Analysis

How to Use It and Why

Glance at the end of any *Cooking Light* recipe, and you'll see how committed we are to helping you make the best of today's light cooking. With chefs, registered dietitians, home economists, and a computer system that analyzes every ingredient we use, *Cooking Light* gives you authoritative dietary detail like no other magazine. We go to such lengths so you can see how our recipes fit into your healthful eating plan. If you're trying to lose weight, the calorie and fat figures will probably help most. But if you're keeping a close eye on the sodium, cholesterol, and saturated fat in your diet, we provide those numbers, too. And because many women don't get enough iron or calcium, we can help there, as well. Finally, there's a fiber analysis for those of us who don't get enough roughage.

Here's a helpful guide to put our nutritional analysis numbers into perspective. Remember, one size doesn't fit all, so take your lifestyle, age, and circumstances into consideration when determining your nutrition needs. For example, pregnant or breast-feeding women need more protein, calories, and calcium. And women older than 50 need 1,200mg of calcium daily, 200mg more than the amount recommended for younger women.

In Our Nutritional Analysis, We Use These Abbreviations

sat	saturated fat	CARB	carbohydrates	g	gram
mono	monounsaturated fat	CHOL	cholesterol	mg	milligram
poly	polyunsaturated fat	CALC	calcium		

Daily Nutrition Guide

	Women ages 25 to 50	Women over 50	Men ages 24 to 50	Men over 50
Calories	2,000	2,000 or less	2,700	2,500
Protein	50g	50g or less	63g	60g
Fat	65g or less	65g or less	88g or less	83g or less
Saturated Fat	20g or less	20g or less	27g or less	25g or less
Carbohydrates	304g	304g	410g	375g
Fiber	25g to 35g	25g to 35g	25g to 35g	25g to 35g
Cholesterol	300mg or less	300mg or less	300mg or less	300mg or less
Iron	18mg	8mg	8mg	8mg
Sodium	2,300mg or less	1,500mg or less	2,300mg or less	1,500mg or less
Calcium	1,000mg	1,200mg	1,000mg	1,000mg

The nutritional values used in our calculations either come from The Food Processor, Version 10.4 (ESHA Research), or are provided by food manufacturers.

Metric Equivalents

The information in the following charts is provided to help cooks outside the United States successfully use the recipes in this book. All equivalents are approximate.

Cooking/Oven Temperatures

	Fahrenheit	Celsius	Gas Mark
Freeze Water	32° F	0° C	
Room Temp.	68° F	20° C	
Boil Water	212° F	100° C	
Bake	325° F	160° C	3
	350° F	180° C	4
	375° F	190° C	5
	400° F	200° C	6
	425° F	220° C	7
	450° F	230° C	8
Broil			Grill

Liquid Ingredients by Volume

¼ tsp	=					1 ml		
½ tsp	=					2 ml		
1 tsp	=					5 ml		
3 tsp	=	1 Tbsp	=	½ fl oz	=	15 ml		
2 Tbsp	=	⅛ cup	=	1 fl oz	=	30 ml		
4 Tbsp	=	¼ cup	=	2 fl oz	=	60 ml		
5⅓ Tbsp	=	⅓ cup	=	3 fl oz	=	80 ml		
8 Tbsp	=	½ cup	=	4 fl oz	=	120 ml		
10⅔ Tbsp	=	⅔ cup	=	5 fl oz	=	160 ml		
12 Tbsp	=	¾ cup	=	6 fl oz	=	180 ml		
16 Tbsp	=	1 cup	=	8 fl oz	=	240 ml		
1 pt	=	2 cups	=	16 fl oz	=	480 ml		
1 qt	=	4 cups	=	32 fl oz	=	960 ml		
				33 fl oz	=	1000 ml	=	1 l

Dry Ingredients by Weight

(To convert ounces to grams, multiply the number of ounces by 30.)

1 oz	=	1/16 lb	=	30 g
4 oz	=	¼ lb	=	120 g
8 oz	=	½ lb	=	240 g
12 oz	=	¾ lb	=	360 g
16 oz	=	1 lb	=	480 g

Length

(To convert inches to centimeters, multiply the number of inches by 2.5.)

1 in	=					2.5 cm		
6 in	=	½ ft			=	15 cm		
12 in	=	1 ft			=	30 cm		
36 in	=	3 ft	=	1 yd	=	90 cm		
40 in	=					100 cm	=	1 m

Equivalents for Different Types of Ingredients

Standard Cup	Fine Powder (ex. flour)	Grain (ex. rice)	Granular (ex. sugar)	Liquid Solids (ex. butter)	Liquid (ex. milk)
1	140 g	150 g	190 g	200 g	240 ml
¾	105 g	113 g	143 g	150 g	180 ml
⅔	93 g	100 g	125 g	133 g	160 ml
½	70 g	75 g	95 g	100 g	120 ml
⅓	47 g	50 g	63 g	67 g	80 ml
¼	35 g	38 g	48 g	50 g	60 ml
⅛	18 g	19 g	24 g	25 g	30 ml

INDEX

ISBN-13: 978-0-8487-3997-3
ISBN-10: 0-8487-3997-3

Library of Congress Control Number: 2013941128
Printed in the United States of America
First Printing 2013

Be sure to check with your health-care provider before making any changes in your diet.

Oxmoor House
Editorial Director: Leah McLaughlin
Creative Director: Felicity Keane
Brand Manager: Michelle Turner Aycock
Senior Editor: Andrea C. Kirkland, MS, RD
Managing Editor: Rebecca Benton

Cooking Light 3-Step Express Meals
Editor: Rachel Quinlivan West, RD
Art Director: Claire Cormany
Director, Test Kitchen: Elizabeth Tyler Austin
Assistant Director, Test Kitchen: Julie Gunter
Recipe Developers and Testers: Wendy Ball, RD; Victoria E. Cox; Tamara Goldis, RD; Stefanie Maloney; Callie Nash; Karen Rankin; Leah Van Deren
Recipe Editor: Alyson Moreland Haynes
Food Stylists: Margaret Monroe Dickey, Catherine Crowell Steele
Photography Director: Jim Bathie
Senior Photographer: Hélène Dujardin
Senior Photo Stylist: Kay E. Clarke
Photo Stylist: Mindi Shapiro Levine
Assistant Photo Stylist: Mary Louise Menendez
Production Managers: Theresa Beste-Farley, Tamara Nall Wilder

Contributors
Editor: Pam Hoenig
Project Editors: Melissa Brown, Jena Hippensteel
Compositor: Dréa Zacharenko
Copy Editors: Adrienne Davis, Jacqueline Giovanelli
Proofreader: Dolores Hydock
Indexer: Mary Ann Laurens
Interns: Susan Kemp, Jeffrey Preis, Maria Sanders, Julia Sayers
Food Stylist: Charlotte Autry
Photographer: Johnny Autry

Cooking Light®
Editor: Scott Mowbray
Executive Managing Editor: Phillip Rhodes
Executive Editor, Food: Ann Taylor Pittman
Executive Editor, Digital: Allison Long Lowery
Special Publications Editor: Mary Simpson Creel, MS, RD
Senior Food Editors: Timothy Q. Cebula, Julianna Grimes
Senior Editor: Cindy Hatcher
Assistant Editor, Nutrition: Sidney Fry, MS, RD
Assistant Editors: Kimberly Holland, Phoebe Wu
Test Kitchen Manager: Tiffany Vickers Davis
Recipe Testers and Developers: Robin Bashinsky, Adam Hickman, Deb Wise
Art Directors: Fernande Bondarenko, Shawna Kalish, Rachel Cardina Lasserre
Senior Designer: Anna Bird
Designer: Hagen Stegall
Assistant Designer: Nicole Gerrity
Acting Photo Director: Julie Claire
Assistant Photo Editor: Amy Delaune
Senior Photographer: Randy Mayor
Senior Prop Stylist: Cindy Barr
Chief Food Stylist: Kellie Gerber Kelley
Food Styling Assistant: Blakeslee Giles
Production Director: Liz Rhoades
Production Editor: Hazel R. Eddins
Copy Director: Susan Roberts
Copy Editor: Kate Johnson
Research Editor: Michelle Gibson Daniels
Administrative Coordinator: Carol D. Johnson
Cookinglight.com Editor: Mallory Daugherty Brasseale
Cookinglight.com Assistant Editor/Producer: Michelle Klug

Time Home Entertainment Inc.
Publisher: Jim Childs
VP, Brand & Digital Strategy: Steven Sandonato
Executive Director, Marketing Services: Carol Pittard
Executive Director, Retail & Special Sales: Tom Mifsud
Director, Bookazine Development & Marketing: Laura Adam
Executive Publishing Director: Joy Butts
Associate Publishing Director: Megan Pearlman
Finance Director: Glenn Buonocore
Associate General Counsel: Helen Wan

To order additional publications, call **1-800-765-6400** or **1-800-491-0551**.

To search, savor, and share thousands of recipes, visit **myrecipes.com**